CHICKEN

CHICKEN

140 ways to baste, braise, roast, grill and
create delicious family meals

This edition published in 2013.

Parragon
Queen Street House
4 Queen Street
Bath
BA1 1HE, UK

ISBN: 978-1-4454-7803-6

Printed in China

Notes for the reader:

All spoon measurements are level.

Unless otherwise stated milk is assumed to be whole and
eggs are medium-size.

Times given are an approximate guide only. Preparation
times differ according to different techniques used by
different people and the cooking times may also vary from
those given as a result of the type of oven used.

Sufferers from nut allergies should be aware that some of the
ready-prepared ingredients used in the recipes in this book
may contain nuts. Always check the packaging before use.

Recipes using raw or very lightly cooked eggs should be
avoided by infants, the elderly, pregnant women,
convalescents, and anyone with a chronic condition.

1

A BIRD IN THE HAND:
APPETIZERS, SNACKS AND WRAPS

Asian-flavored chicken wings now rival the venerable Buffalo-style in popularity, and this sticky, spicy, garlicky version is my favorite.

spicy ginger-garlic wings

serves 4–6

4 pounds chicken wings

1 tablespoon vegetable oil

1 teaspoon salt

1 tablespoon all-purpose flour

For the sauce:

4 crushed garlic cloves, peeled, finely minced

2 tablespoons freshly grated ginger

¼ teaspoon red chile flakes, or to taste

½ cup rice vinegar

½ cup packed dark brown sugar

1 teaspoon soy sauce

Preheat oven to 425°F.

If the chicken wings being used were frozen and thawed, be sure they're completely dry before starting recipe. If using whole wings, cut each into two pieces (in wing-speak called the "flat" and the "drum"). The small wing tips can be discarded, or saved for stock. In a large mixing bowl, toss the wings with the oil and salt. Add the flour, and toss until evenly coated.

Line two heavy-duty baking sheets with lightly greased foil or silicon baking mats. Divide the wings, and spread out evenly. Do not crowd. Bake for 25 minutes, remove, and turn the wings over. Return to the oven, and cook another 20–30 minutes, or until the wings are well browned and cooked through.

Note: Cooking times will vary based on size of the wings. When fully cooked, the bones will easily pull out from the meat.

While the wings are baking, mix all the sauce ingredients in a saucepan. Bring to a simmer, whisking, over medium heat. Remove from heat, and reserve.

After the wings are cooked, transfer to a large mixing bowl. Pour the warm sauce over the hot wings, and toss with a spoon or spatula to completely coat. Let rest for 10 minutes, and toss again. The glaze will get sticky and thicken slightly as it cools.

Serve warm or at room temperature.

America's favorite appetizer is usually deep-fried, but this delicious home version uses a very hot oven instead.

buffalo chicken wings

makes 40 pieces

4 pounds chicken wings

1 tablespoon vegetable oil

1 tablespoon all-purpose flour

1 teaspoon salt

1 tablespoon all-purpose flour

For the sauce:

²/₃ cup Frank's RedHot® sauce

8 tablespoons (1 stick) cold unsalted butter, cut into 1-inch slices

1½ tablespoons distilled white vinegar

¼ teaspoon Worcestershire sauce

1 teaspoon Tabasco

¼ teaspoon cayenne pepper

Pinch of garlic powder

Salt, to taste

Celery sticks and blue cheese dressing, for serving

Preheat oven to 425°F.

If the chicken wings being used were frozen and thawed, be sure they're completely dry before starting recipe. If using whole wings, cut each into two pieces (in wing-speak, called the "flat" and the "drum"). The small wing tips can be discarded, or saved for stock. In a large mixing bowl, toss the wings with the oil, salt, and flour until evenly coated

Line two heavy-duty baking sheets with lightly greased foil or silicon baking mats. Divide the wings, and spread out evenly. Do not crowd. Bake for 25 minutes, remove, and turn the wings over. Return to the oven, and cook another 20–30 minutes, or until the wings are well browned and cooked through.

Note: Cooking times will vary, based on size of the wings. When fully cooked, the bones will easily pull out from the meat.

While the wings are baking, mix all the sauce ingredients in a saucepan. Bring to a simmer, whisking over medium heat. Remove from heat, and reserve. Taste sauce; adjust for salt and spiciness, if desired.

After the wings are cooked, transfer to a large mixing bowl. Pour the warm sauce over the hot wings, and toss with a spoon or spatula to completely coat. Let rest 5 minutes, toss again, and serve immediately with celery sticks and blue cheese dressing on the side.

spicy ginger-garlic wings

❖

page 8

buffalo chicken wings

❧

page 9

Croquettes are more popular in Europe than here in the States, which is sort of a mystery since they are so delicious—and perfect for shredded chicken.

chicken croquettes

makes 12 croquettes

4 tablespoons (½ stick) butter

½ onion, finely diced

3 tablespoons all-purpose flour

1¼ cups whole milk

1 teaspoon salt

Pinch of ground nutmeg

2 cups finely shredded cooked chicken

½ teaspoon paprika

2 teaspoon minced chives

2 large eggs, beaten

Plain bread crumbs, as needed

Vegetable oil, for frying

Heat butter in a heavy skillet over medium heat. Add the onion and sauté until translucent, about 4 minutes. Add flour, and cook stirring for 4 minutes more.

Add milk gradually, whisking continuously. Cook, stirring until the sauce boils, and has reduced and become quite thick. Turn off heat, and stir in salt, nutmeg, chicken, paprika, and chives. Once mixed, remove and allow to cool to room temperature. Transfer to a bowl and refrigerate for at least 6 hours, or overnight.

Dampen to your hands with cold water, and roll about ¼ cup of the mixture into a cylindrical-shaped log with your hands. Repeat to make about 12.

Roll croquettes in eggs, then in the breadcrumbs. Let rest 10 minutes before frying. Fry in vegetable oil until browned on all sides, about 3 minutes per side. Serve immediately.

These quick and easy Mediterranean-style sandwiches feature the great combo of hot, spicy chicken and a cool refreshing yogurt sauce.

spicy chicken pitas

serves 4

For the sauce:

1 clove garlic, minced

1 teaspoon lemon zest

1 tablespoon lemon juice

½ cup plain yogurt

¼ teaspoon hot sauce or to taste

½ cup grated English cucumber

¼ cup chopped fresh flat-leaf parsley

For the filling:

1 small onion, sliced very thin

1 pound boneless, skinless chicken breasts, cut into thin strips

½ teaspoon dried oregano

¼ teaspoon cayenne pepper

⅛ teaspoon cinnamon

Salt, to taste

1 tablespoon olive oil

4 pita or flatbreads, cut in half

In a small bowl, stir together the sauce ingredients. Let stand 15 minutes.

Add all the filling ingredients to a mixing bowl, and mix well. Heat a large skillet over high heat. When very hot, add the mixture, and sauté for 5 minutes, or until chicken is cooked through.

Fill pita halves with chicken, and spoon in the yogurt sauce. Serve immediately.

Any kid will tell you that crispy chicken fingers rule! Make a batch of these, and watch how fast they disappear.

crispy chicken fingers

makes 8 pieces

1 cup all-purpose flour

2 teaspoons salt

1 teaspoon garlic salt

½ teaspoon white pepper

4 large boneless, skinless chicken breasts, cut into ½-inch strips

4 eggs, beaten

1 tablespoon whole milk

2½ cups Japanese-style panko breadcrumbs

¾ cup finely grated Parmesan

Canola oil, for frying

Add the flour, salt, garlic salt, and white pepper into a large, sealable plastic freezer bag. Shake to mix. Add the chicken strips, seal the bag, and shake vigorously to coat evenly with flour.

In a mixing bowl, whisk together the eggs and milk. Add the chicken strips, shaking off the excess flour as you remove them from the bag. Stir until the strips are complete coated in the egg.

Mix the breadcrumbs and grated cheese together in a shallow pan. Use one hand to remove the chicken strips from the bowl of eggs, a few at a time, allowing the excess egg to drip off, and place in the pan of panko. Use the other hand to coat the chicken in the breadcrumbs and cheese, pressing them in firmly. As they are breaded, place the strips on baking sheets or racks. When done breading, let the chicken strips rest for 10 minutes before frying.

Pour about ½ inch of oil in a large, heavy skillet (ideally cast-iron) and set over medium-high heat. When the oil is hot enough to fry (350–375°F, or test with a small piece of breading), cook for 2–3 minutes per side, or until golden-brown and cooked through. Work in batches, drain on paper towels or baking rack, and keep the cooked chicken fingers in a warm oven (175°F) until the rest are done. Serve with your favorite dipping sauce.

This healthy and delicious chicken recipe is a snap using a cooked rotisserie and jarred salsa. The contrast between the crisp, cold lettuce cups and the spicy, stewed chicken is wonderful. This chicken recipe can be served as an appetizer or a main course.

spicy chicken lettuce cups

makes about 12 lettuce cups

1 whole roasted chicken, bones, fat, and skin removed, meat shredded

2 cups jarred spicy-style red salsa

½ cup chopped green onions

1 teaspoon ground cumin

Salt and pepper, to taste

2 heads butter lettuce, washed, separated into leaves

½ bunch cilantro, chopped

Add all the ingredients except the lettuce and cilantro into a saucepan, and place over medium-low heat. Bring to a low simmer, and cook for 10 minutes. Allow mixture to cool to just warm or room temperature. Taste, and adjust seasoning. Spoon into each of the lettuce leaves, and top with fresh cilantro.

These are great for an anytime snack, but also perfect for entertaining. Feel free to change the cranberry to any other fruit jelly for countless variations.

chicken meatballs
with orange-cranberry glaze

makes 36 cocktail meatballs

For the meatballs:

1¼ pound ground chicken

¼ teaspoon poultry seasoning

1 teaspoon salt

1 teaspoon onion powder

½ teaspoon garlic salt

½ teaspoon freshly ground black pepper

¼ teaspoon Worcestershire sauce

Pinch of cayenne pepper

1 large egg, beaten

¼ cup milk

½ cup plain bread crumbs

For the glaze:

1 cup canned jellied cranberry sauce

½ cup orange jelly or marmalade

½ cup chicken broth or water

1 tablespoon minced jalapeño peppers, optional

1 tablespoon minced Fresno peppers, optional

Salt and freshly ground black pepper, to taste

1 tablespoon vegetable oil

To make the meatballs: Add all the meatball ingredients to a mixing bowl and stir until thoroughly combined. Refrigerate for at least 1 hour before rolling into small cocktail-sized meatballs (about 36).

To make the glaze: Whisk together the glaze ingredients in a bowl. Don't worry about getting the mixture completely smooth, as it will melt and become uniform in the pan when heated with the meatballs.

Brown the meatballs on all sides in the vegetable oil, using a large non-stick skillet over medium heat. Once browned, add the glaze mixture and bring to a boil. Cook, stirring often, for 10 minutes, or until the glaze has thickened and the meatballs are cooked through.

Serve immediately (with toothpicks on the side), or hold over low heat in a chafing dish.

Any party's snack table would benefit from this simple, delicious nacho-cheese chip dip. You can mix this up the day before and bake right before guests arrive.

chicken nacho dip

serves 8

1 tablespoon vegetable oil

3 boneless, skinless chicken breasts, cut into ¼-inch cubes

2 cloves garlic, minced

1 bunch green onions, light parts only, chopped

8 ounces cream cheese

1 cup sour cream

¾ cup spicy jarred salsa

8 ounces shredded Monterey Jack cheese

4 ounces shredded Cheddar cheese

Bag of corn tortilla chips

Preheat oven to 375°F.

In a skillet, heat the vegetable oil over medium-high heat. Add the chicken, garlic, and green onions, and cook, stirring for about 6–7 minutes until the chicken is just cooked through.

Transfer into a mixing bowl, and add the remaining ingredients. Mix well, and spread mixture into a 2-quart baking dish. Bake about 15–20 minutes, or until browned and bubbling. Serve warm with chips.

chicken meatballs
with orange-cranberry glaze

✣

page 20

chicken nacho dip

page 21

These chicken nuggets taste like the ones from a certain popular fast-food chain, except they require about 20 fewer ingredients.

chicken nuggets

serves 6

1 large egg

1 cup water

1 cup flour

¼ teaspoon white pepper

⅛ teaspoon garlic powder

2 teaspoons salt

1 teaspoon onion powder

1½ pounds boneless, skinless chicken breasts

canola oil for deep frying

Beat egg and water in a mixing bowl and reserve.

Combine dry ingredients in a plastic bag. Cut chicken into bite-sized pieces and add to bag. Shake to coat with flour.

Remove the chicken pieces from the bag and toss to coat in egg mixture. Return to bag of flour, and shake again to coat. Put the bag containing the chicken into the freezer for 1 hour.

Remove the chicken from the bag, shake off excess flour, and deep-fry in preheated 375°F oil until golden-brown. Drain on paper towels, and serve immediately.

This flat yet flavorsome Italian bread may resemble a pizza base, but is substantial enough to be split in two horizontally and filled with anything you like to make a delicious sandwich.

smoked chicken and ham focaccia

serves 2-4

1 thick focaccia loaf

Handful of fresh basil leaves

2 small zucchini, coarsely shredded

6 wafer-thin slices of smoked chicken

6 wafer-thin slices of cooked ham

8 ounces Taleggio cheese, cut into strips

Freshly grated nutmeg (optional)

Cherry tomatoes and salad leaves, to serve

Preheat a grill pan under the broiler until both broiler and grill pan are hot. If you do not have a grill pan, heat a heavy baking sheet or roasting pan instead. Slice the focaccia in half horizontally and cut the top half lengthwise into strips.

Cover the bottom half of the focaccia with an even layer of the grated zucchini, then cover with the basil leaves. Cover this with the chicken and ham. Lay the strips of focaccia on top, placing strips of cheese between them. Sprinkle with a little nutmeg, if using.

Place the assembled bread on the preheated grill pan and cook under the broiler, well away from the heat, for about 5 minutes, until the cheese has melted, and the top of the bread is browned. Cut the focaccia into four pieces and serve immediately with cherry tomatoes and salad leaves.

Crostini, bruschetta, or just plain toasts—whatever you call them, this is a delicious way to serve up a substantial chicken snack, Mediterranean style.

chicken toasts

serves 4

12 slices of French bread or country bread

¼ cup olive oil

2 garlic cloves, chopped

2 tablespoons finely chopped fresh oregano, plus extra to garnish

3½ ounces cold roast chicken, cut into small, thin slices

4 tomatoes, sliced

12 thin slices of goat cheese

12 black olives, pitted and chopped

Salt and pepper

Preheat the broiler to medium. Put the bread under the broiler and lightly toast on both sides.

Meanwhile, pour the oil into a bowl and add the garlic and oregano. Season with salt and pepper and mix well. Remove the toasted bread slices from the broiler and brush them on one side only with a little of the oil mixture.

Preheat the oven to 350°F. Place the bread slices, oiled sides up, on a baking sheet. Put some of the sliced chicken on top of each one, followed by a slice of tomato.

Divide the slices of goat cheese among the bread slices, then top with the olives.

Drizzle over the remaining oil mixture and transfer to the preheated oven. Bake for about 5 minutes, or until the cheese is golden and starting to melt. Garnish with oregano and serve immediately.

This crunchy peanut sauce has a kick of chile to add some spice to this classic dish.

chicken satay skewers
with peanut sauce

serves 4

4 boneless, skinless chicken breasts (about 6 ounces each), cut into 1-inch cubes

¼ cup soy sauce

1 tablespoon cornstarch

2 garlic cloves, finely chopped

1-inch piece fresh ginger, peeled and finely chopped

¼ cup cucumber, coarsely chopped, to serve

For the peanut sauce:

2 tablespoons peanut or vegetable oil

½ onion, finely chopped

1 garlic clove, finely chopped

¼ cup chunky peanut butter

¼ cup water

½ teaspoon chile powder

Put the chicken cubes in a shallow dish. Mix the soy sauce, cornstarch, garlic, and ginger together in a small bowl, and pour over the chicken. Cover and let marinate in the refrigerator for at least 2 hours.

Meanwhile, soak 12 bamboo skewers in cold water for at least 30 minutes. Preheat the broiler.

Thread the chicken pieces onto the bamboo skewers. Transfer the skewers to a broiler pan, and cook under the preheated broiler for 3–4 minutes. Turn the skewers over, and cook for an additional 3–4 minutes, or until cooked through.

Meanwhile, to make the sauce, heat the oil in a saucepan, add the onion and garlic, and cook over medium heat, stirring frequently, for 3–4 minutes until softened.

Add the peanut butter, water, and chile powder, and simmer for 2–3 minutes, until softened and thinned. Serve the skewers immediately with the warm sauce and cucumber.

If there's an easier and more enjoyable snack than a cheesy quesadilla, we don't know what that is. This version features the south-of-the-border kick of poblano peppers.

chicken, mushroom and poblano quesadilla

serves 8

2 tablespoons vegetable oil, divided

1 onion, diced

1 poblano pepper, seeded, cut into thin strips

4 large button mushrooms, sliced thin

2 boneless, skinless chicken breasts, cut into ¼-inch cubes

¼ teaspoon chipotle chile powder

Salt and freshly ground black pepper, to taste

½ cup shredded Cheddar cheese

½ cup shredded Monterey Jack cheese

Eight 10-inch flour tortillas

Preheat oven to 375°F.

In a large skillet, heat 1 tablespoon oil over medium-high heat. Add onions and peppers and cook for 3–4 minutes or until the vegetables begin to soften. Add the chicken and chipotle, and sauté until the chicken is cooked through and the onions are golden brown. Season with salt and pepper to taste.

Grease baking sheets with the remaining oil. Place four tortillas down and top with the chicken-onion mixture, followed by the Cheddar and Monterey Jack cheeses. Top with remaining tortillas. Place layered tortillas on a large baking sheet. Bake for 15–20 minutes, or until cheese is melted. Remove, let cool 5 minutes, cut into quarters, and serve.

A healthy yet totally delicious alternative to the classic beef version, this amazing burger scores low on fat and high on taste.

the ultimate chicken burger

serves 4

4 large boneless, skinless chicken breasts (about 6 ounces each)

1 large egg white

1 tablespoon cornstarch

1 tablespoon all-purpose flour

1 egg, beaten

1 cup fresh white breadcrumbs

2 tablespoons corn oil

2 large tomatoes, sliced

Pinch of salt

Freshly ground black pepper

To serve:

4 burger buns, sliced

Shredded lettuce

Mayonnaise

Salt and pepper, to taste

French fries

Place the chicken breasts between 2 sheets of nonstick parchment paper and flatten slightly using a meat mallet or a rolling pin. Beat the egg white and cornstarch together, and brush over the chicken. Cover, and let chill for 30 minutes, and then coat in the flour.

Place the egg and breadcrumbs in 2 separate bowls. Coat the burgers first in the egg, allowing any excess to drip back into the bowl, and then in the breadcrumbs.

Heat a heavy-bottom skillet, and add the oil. When hot, add the burgers, and cook over medium heat for 6–8 minutes on each side, or until thoroughly cooked. If you are in doubt, cut one of the burgers in half. If there is any sign of pinkness, cook for a little longer. Add the tomato slices for the last 1–2 minutes of the cooking time to heat through.

Place the burgers in the burger buns with the tomato slices, a little shredded lettuce and a spoonful of mayonnaise. Season to taste with salt and pepper, and serve with French fries.

chicken, mushroom and
poblano quesadilla
❖
page 32

the ultimate chicken burger

page 33

There's nothing like sitting on the couch, watching a great movie, munching on a bowl of "popcorn" chicken. Okay, so maybe it's not as traditional, but it is delicious!

"popcorn" chicken

serves 4

1 pound boneless, skinless chicken breasts, diced into bite-size ½-inch pieces

1 teaspoon honey

2 teaspoons salt

1 egg, beaten

½ cup whole milk

½ teaspoon freshly ground black pepper

½ teaspoon paprika

¼ teaspoon cayenne pepper

1 cup all-purpose flour, or as needed

Vegetable oil, for deep-frying

In a mixing bowl, toss the chicken pieces with the honey and ½ teaspoon of salt. Let sit for 15 minutes. In another mixing bowl, mix together egg and milk.

In a large plastic freezer bag combine remaining salt, pepper, spices and flour. Seal and shake to combine.

Add the chicken pieces to the egg and milk. Stir to combine. Remove with a slotted spoon, and transfer to the bag of seasoned flour. Seal bag, and shake vigorously to combine.

Let chicken stay in the flour mixture for about 12–15 minutes while you heat the frying oil. In a large heavy pot or cast-iron pan, heat about 1 inch of oil to 375°F. Shake excess flour off of the chicken, and fry until golden-brown, about 4 minutes. Cook in batches, if necessary.

Once cooked, transfer with a slotted spoon to a paper towel–lined platter. Sprinkle with more salt, if desired. Serve immediately with your favorite dipping sauce.

The buttermilk not only keeps the chicken moist and tender, but it also helps create the irresistibly crisp, crunchy coating.

buttermilk fried chicken

makes 8 pieces

For the marinade:

1 whole chicken (about 4 pounds),
cut into 8 serving-size pieces

1 teaspoon salt

1 teaspoon black pepper

1 teaspoon paprika

½ teaspoon cayenne pepper

½ teaspoon white pepper

1 teaspoon poultry seasoning

2 cups buttermilk

For the seasoned flour:

2 cups all-purpose flour

1 tablespoon salt

1 teaspoon black pepper

1 teaspoon paprika

¼ teaspoon cayenne pepper

½ teaspoon white pepper

1 teaspoon garlic salt

1 teaspoon onion powder

2 quarts peanut oil or vegetable
shortening for frying

Place the chicken in a large glass bowl or plastic container. Add all the seasonings, and toss to coat very thoroughly. Pour over the buttermilk. Use tongs to move the chicken pieces around until they are coated. Cover and refrigerate for 6 to 12 hours.

Mix together the seasoned flour ingredients in a large baking dish. Drain the chicken pieces in a colander, and toss into the flour. Toss to coat the chicken completely with the flour mixture. Make sure it's thoroughly covered, including all the nooks and crannies. Gently shake off excess flour, and reserve on a plate.

Heat the oil or shortening in a heavy Dutch oven to 350°F. Carefully add the chicken, and fry for 10 minutes. Use tongs or a wire strainer to turn the pieces over, and continue cook for another approximately 8–10 minutes, or until crisp and golden-brown, and the chicken has reached an internal temperature of 175–180°F.

Remove to drain on a wire rack for 5 minutes before serving. Sprinkle with additional salt and/or hot pepper, if desired.

Everything you like about Buffalo chicken wings—without the bones! This hot dip is the perfect party food and a great way to use up leftover chicken.

buffalo chicken dip

serves 8

1 tablespoon olive oil

1 cup diced celery

One 8-ounce package cream cheese

1 cup blue cheese dressing

½ cup ranch dressing

2 cups diced cooked chicken

¼ cup Frank's RedHot® pepper sauce, or other similar brand

1 cup shredded white Cheddar cheese

Preheat oven to 350°F.

Heat olive oil in a wide skillet over medium heat. Add celery and cook for 3 minutes, or until almost tender. Stir in cream cheese and dressings. Turn to low, and cook, stirring, until soft and combined. Stir in the chicken and hot sauce.

Spoon mixture into a 2-quart baking dish. Sprinkle with the Cheddar cheese, and bake for 30 minutes, or until golden and bubbling.

This crunchy but creamy wrap filling could have been invented to use up all that leftover chicken, although it's so delicious you'll want to cook it from scratch.

chicken wraps

makes 4 wraps

⅔ cup plain yogurt

1 tablespoon whole-grain mustard

10 ounces cooked boneless, skinless chicken breasts, diced

5 ounces iceberg lettuce, finely shredded

3 ounces cucumber, thinly sliced

2 celery stalks, sliced

½ cup red seedless grapes, halved

4 large flour tortillas

Pepper

Combine the yogurt and mustard in a bowl and season to taste with pepper. Stir in the chicken and toss until thoroughly coated.

Put the lettuce, cucumber, celery, and grapes into a separate bowl and mix well.

Fold a tortilla in half and in half again to make a cone that is easy to hold. Half-fill the tortilla pocket with a quarter of the salad mixture and top with a quarter of the chicken mixture. Repeat with the remaining tortillas, salad, and chicken. Serve immediately.

The ultimate lunch to go, bursting with fresh flavor and so tasty you just might not want to slice and share it!

chicken-stuffed baguette

serves 1-2

1 garlic clove, halved

1 large baguette, sliced lengthwise

½ cup olive oil

2 ounces cold roast chicken, thinly sliced

Fresh basil leaves

2 large tomatoes, sliced

¾ ounce canned anchovy fillets, drained

8 large pitted black olives, chopped

Pepper

Rub the garlic over the insides of the baguette and sprinkle with the oil.

Arrange the chicken on top of the bread. Scatter the basil leaves over the chicken. Place the tomatoes and anchovies on top of the chicken.

Scatter with the black olives, and season with plenty of pepper. Sandwich the baguette back together and wrap tightly in foil until required. Cut into slices to serve.

That's right—a bacon, lettuce, and tomato pizza! If you like the sandwich, you'll love the chicken pizza version.

BLT chicken pizza

serves 4

1 prepared pizza dough, enough for one 15-inch round pizza

²/₃ cup jarred pizza sauce, or enough to cover

½ cup crumbled cooked bacon

8 ounces shredded white Cheddar cheese

4 ounces shredded mozzarella cheese

1 cup diced or shredded cooked chicken, from leftover roast or rotisserie chicken

1 cup sweet cherry tomatoes, halved

Large handful baby arugula, washed and dried

2 teaspoons olive oil

Salt and pepper, to taste

Preheat oven to 450°F.

Roll out dough on a lightly floured surface to approximately a 15-inch circle. Place on a large metal pizza pan. Spread pizza sauce over evenly. Sprinkle over bacon. Sprinkle over cheeses. Top with chicken and cherry tomatoes.

Bake for 10–12 minutes, or until cheese is bubbling and crust is browned.

Remove from oven and let cool slightly. While pizza is cooling, toss arugula with olive oil, and season with salt and pepper to taste. Scatter over pizza, cut, and serve immediately.

Using salsa instead of the usual pizza sauce is a great trick. You'll be surprised how many of your guests can't figure out your "secret ingredient."

chicken, onion and smoked-ham pizza

serves 4

1 prepared pizza dough, enough for one 15-inch round pizza

²/₃ cup jarred roasted-tomato salsa, or enough to cover pizza

6 ounces shredded mozzarella cheese

1 cup diced or shredded chicken, from leftover roast or rotisserie chicken

½ cup diced smoked ham

½ sweet onion, thinly sliced

6 ounces shredded white Cheddar cheese

2 tablespoons fresh chopped flat-leaf parsley

Preheat oven to 450°F.

Roll out dough on a lightly floured surface to approximately a 15-inch circle. Place on a large metal pizza pan.

Spread salsa over dough evenly. Scatter over the mozzarella. Scatter over chicken, ham and sweet onion evenly. Top with Cheddar cheese.

Bake for 10–12 minutes or until cheese is bubbling and crust is browned.

Remove from oven and let cool slightly. Sprinkle with chopped cilantro and fresh parsley. Cut and serve immediately.

Nothing beats pizza night. Period.

chicken and mushroom pizza

serves 2-4

¼ cup olive oil, plus extra for brushing

2 shallots, thinly sliced

1 yellow bell pepper, seeded and cut into thin strips

½ cup mushrooms, thinly sliced

12 ounces boneless, skinless chicken breasts, cut into thin strips

Pinch of salt

Freshly ground black pepper

One 10-inch pizza crust

2 tablespoons chopped fresh flat-leaf parsley

1½ cups grated mozzarella cheese

Preheat the oven to 400°F.

Brush a baking sheet with oil.

Heat 2 tablespoons of olive oil in a wok or large skillet. Add the shallots, bell pepper, mushrooms, and chicken, and stir-fry over medium-high heat for 4–5 minutes. Season to taste. Remove the mixture with a slotted spoon and let cool.

Brush the pizza crust with 1 tablespoon of olive oil. Stir the parsley into the chicken-mushroom mixture, and spread it evenly over the pizza crust almost to the edge. Sprinkle with the mozzarella, drizzle over the remaining olive oil, and bake for 20 minutes, until the edge is crisp and golden. Serve immediately.

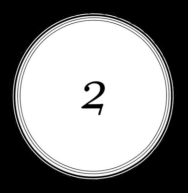

2

CHICKEN SALADS

This sweet, crunchy classic is named for the Waldorf Astoria Hotel in New York City, where it was first created. Poached chicken only makes it better.

chicken waldorf salad

serves 6

3 boneless, skinless chicken breasts

1 bay leaf

½ teaspoon salt

¾ cup raw walnut halves

⅓ cup mayonnaise

2 tablespoons freshly squeezed lemon juice

1 tablespoon plain yogurt

Freshly ground black pepper, to taste

3 large apples, cored, cut into 1-inch chunks

1 cup green or red seedless grape halves

⅔ cup sliced celery, about ¼-inch thick

1 small head butter lettuce

Place the chicken breasts, bay leaf, and salt in a saucepan. Cover with enough water just to cover. Bring to a simmer over medium-high heat. Turn heat to low, cover, and cook for 12 minutes, or until chicken is cooked through. Remove chicken, allow to cool, and refrigerate until needed. When ready to serve, cut into 1-inch cubes.

Preheat oven to 350°F. Arrange walnuts on a baking sheet, and bake for 8 minutes. Let cool on a cutting board, roughly chop, and reserve.

Add the mayonnaise, lemon juice, yogurt, salt, and a few grinds of black pepper to a large mixing bowl. Whisk to combine thoroughly. Use a spatula to fold in the apples, grapes, celery, walnuts, and chicken. Mix until evenly coated with the dressing.

Lay down a few lettuce leaves on each plate and spoon the salad over the top. Serve immediately.

America's most famous "composed" salad was invented at Los Angeles' Brown Derby restaurant in 1937. The ingredients are traditionally arranged in neat rows on top of the greens, but it's just as delicious if everything's tossed together.

cobb salad

serves 6

8 slices bacon

4 large handfuls mixed baby greens or other lettuce, torn into bite-size pieces

3 hard-boiled eggs, peeled, chopped

4 cups cooked chicken breast, cubed

2 avocados, peeled, pitted, cubed

1 cup cherry tomatoes, halved

4 ounces Roquefort cheese, crumbled

½ teaspoon Dijon mustard

¼ cup red-wine vinegar

1 teaspoon Worcestershire sauce

1 garlic clove, crushed into a paste

¼ teaspoon salt

¼ teaspoon freshly ground black pepper

$^1/_3$ cup olive oil

Cook the bacon until crisp, drain on paper towels, and when cool enough to handle, crumble and set aside.

Arrange a bed of lettuce in shallow bowls. Arrange the eggs, bacon, chicken, avocados, tomatoes, and Roquefort cheese in rows on top of the lettuce, covering the surface completely.

In a bowl, whisk together the mustard, vinegar, Worcestershire sauce, garlic, salt, and pepper. Slowly drizzle in the olive oil, whisking constantly, to form the dressing. Drizzle the dressing evenly over the salad, and serve immediately.

Curry is a natural with chicken, and while great hot and spicy, it's also perfect in the form of a cold salad. A cooked rotisserie chicken from the market is perfect for this.

curried chicken salad

serves 6

For the dressing:

1 cup mayonnaise

2 tablespoons prepared mango chutney

1 tablespoon curry powder, or to taste

1 teaspoon cumin

Juice of 1 lemon

Juice of 1 lime

2 teaspoons soy sauce

Salt and pepper, to taste

For the salad:

1 large rotisserie chicken, meat picked and roughly chopped (about 4 cups)

2 cups seedless grapes, halved

2 green onions, chopped

¾ cup diced celery

⅓ cup slivered almonds

¼ cup diced red bell pepper

Combine dressing ingredients, mix well and reserve.

Combine chicken-salad ingredients in a large mixing bowl. Add dressing and stir to combine. Chill for at least 1 hour, and serve.

cobb salad

❧

page 54

curried chicken salad

❧

page 55

This classic deli-style chicken salad is begging to be put on some rye toast and served with a big scoop of potato salad. Don't forget the pickles.

deli chicken salad

serves 4

½ cup mayonnaise

1 tablespoon fresh lemon juice

1 teaspoon Dijon mustard

2½ cups chopped cooked chicken meat

1 stalk celery, diced small

1 green onion, minced

Pinch of dried thyme

Pinch of cayenne

Salt and pepper, to taste

Mix all ingredients together thoroughly in a mixing bowl. Wrap and refrigerate for at least 2 hours. Mix again and serve.

With its festive colors and ingredients like dried cranberries and nuts, this chicken salad is perfect for the holidays.

'tis the season chicken salad

serves 10

¾ cup mayonnaise

1 tablespoon fresh lemon juice

⅛ teaspoon cayenne pepper

1 cup dried cranberries

⅔ cup chopped celery

¼ cup minced red bell pepper

¼ cup minced green bell pepper

2 scallions, chopped

½ cup chopped pecans

½ cup chopped walnuts

4 cups cubed, cooked chicken meat

Salt and pepper, to taste

In a mixing bowl, whisk mayonnaise and lemon juice with cayenne and salt. Add cranberries, celery, bell peppers, scallions, pecans, and walnuts. Add chicken, and mix well. Season with salt and pepper, to taste. Chill at least 2 hours before serving.

A hearty salad bursting with the unmistakable flavor of the traditional mild spices used in Louisiana Cajun cooking.

cajun chicken salad

serves 4

4 boneless, skinless chicken breasts (about 6 ounces each)

4 teaspoons Cajun seasoning

2 teaspoons corn oil

1 ripe mango, peeled, pitted, and cut into thick slices

8 ounces mixed salad greens

1 red onion, halved and thinly sliced

1¼ cups diced, cooked beets

½ cup radishes, sliced

½ cup walnut halves

2 tablespoons sesame seeds

For the dressing:

¼ cup walnut oil

1–2 teaspoons whole grain mustard

1 tablespoon lemon juice

Pinch of salt

Freshly ground black pepper, to taste

Make 3 diagonal slashes across each chicken breast. Put the chicken into a shallow dish, and sprinkle all over with the Cajun seasoning. Cover, and chill for at least 30 minutes.

When ready to cook, brush a stovetop grill pan with the corn oil. Heat over high heat until very hot and a few drops of water sprinkled into the pan sizzle immediately. Add the chicken and cook for 7–8 minutes on each side, or until thoroughly cooked. If still slightly pink in the center, cook a little longer. Remove the chicken and set aside.

Add the mango slices to the pan, and cook for 2 minutes on each side. Remove and set aside.

Meanwhile, place the salad greens in a large bowl. Sprinkle the onions, beets, radishes, and walnuts over the greens.

To make the dressing, put the walnut oil, mustard, lemon juice, and salt and pepper to taste in a screw-top jar, and shake until well blended. Pour over the salad, and sprinkle with the sesame seeds.

Cut the reserved chicken into thick slices. Arrange the mango slices on a serving plate. Top with the salad, reserving some of the greens. Place chicken slices on top of the salad and scatter remaining greens over the top.

Chicken paired with cranberry is nothing unusual; but use succulent smoked chicken, then add avocados and crunchy walnuts, and toss it all in a flavor-infused dressing and you'll lift this salad right into the luxury class.

smoked chicken and cranberry salad

serves 4

One 3-pound smoked chicken, whole

1 cup dried cranberries

2 tablespoons apple juice or water

1 pound 4 ounces (3 cups) sugar-snap peas

2 ripe avocados

Juice of ½ lemon

4 lettuce hearts

1 bunch of watercress, trimmed

3 cups arugula

4 ounces (1 cup) walnuts, chopped,
to garnish (optional)

For the dressing:

2 tablespoons olive oil

1 tablespoon walnut oil

2 tablespoons lemon juice

1 tablespoon chopped fresh mixed herbs,
such as parsley and lemon thyme

Salt and pepper, to taste

Carve the chicken carefully, slicing the white meat. Divide the legs into thighs and drumsticks, and trim the wings. Cover with plastic wrap and refrigerate.

Put the cranberries in a bowl. Stir in the apple juice or water, then cover with plastic wrap and let soak for 30 minutes.

Meanwhile, blanch the sugar-snap peas, and then refresh under cold running water and drain.

Peel, pit, and slice the avocados into a bowl, and toss with lemon juice to prevent browning.

Separate the lettuce hearts, and arrange on a large serving platter with the avocados, peas, watercress, arugula, and chicken.

Put all the dressing ingredients, including salt and pepper, to taste, in a screw-top jar, screw on the lid, and then shake until well blended.

Drain the cranberries, mix them with the dressing, and then pour over the salad.

Serve immediately, scattered with walnuts, if using.

cajon chicken salad

⚜

page 62

smoked chicken and cranberry salad
❖
page 63

Quick, easy, nutritious and delicious—this is the perfect meal in minutes.

penne with chicken and feta

serves 4

2 tablespoons olive oil

1 pound boneless, skinless chicken breasts, cut into thin strips

6 scallions, chopped

1 cup feta cheese, diced

¼ cup snipped fresh chives

Salt and freshly ground black pepper, to taste

1 pound dried penne

Heat the olive oil in a heavy-bottom skillet. Add the chicken, and cook over medium heat, stirring frequently, for 5–8 minutes, or until golden all over and cooked through. Add the scallions, and cook for 2 minutes. Stir the feta cheese into the skillet with half the chives, and season to taste with salt and pepper.

Meanwhile, bring a large, heavy-bottomed pan of lightly salted water to a boil. Add the pasta, return to a boil, and cook for 8–10 minutes, or according to the package directions, until tender but still firm to the bite. Drain well, and then transfer to a warmed serving dish.

Spoon the chicken mixture onto the pasta, toss lightly, and serve immediately, garnished with the remaining chives.

Quick and simple to make, this dish can be made in advance and stored in an airtight container in the refrigerator until needed. It's perfect for a summer picnic.

honey and chicken pasta salad

serves 4

For the dressing:

3 tablespoons olive oil

1 tablespoon sherry vinegar

2 teaspoons honey

1 tablespoon fresh thyme leaves

Salt and pepper, to taste

1 cup dried fusilli pasta

2 tablespoons olive oil

1 onion, thinly sliced

1 garlic clove, crushed

1 pound boneless, skinless chicken breasts, thinly sliced

2 tablespoons whole grain mustard

2 tablespoons honey

10 cherry tomatoes, halved

Handful of arugula leaves

Fresh thyme leaves, to garnish

To make the dressing, whisk the dressing ingredients together in a bowl.

Bring a large pan of lightly salted water to a boil. Add the pasta and return to a boil. Cook for 10–12 minutes, or according to the package directions, until just tender.

Meanwhile, heat the oil in a large skillet. Add the onion and garlic, and cook for 5 minutes. Add the chicken and cook, stirring frequently, for 3–4 minutes, until just cooked through. Stir the mustard and honey into the pan, and cook for another 2–3 minutes, until the chicken and onion are golden-brown and sticky.

Drain the pasta, and transfer to a serving bowl. Pour the dressing over it, and toss well. Stir in the chicken and onion, and let cool.

Gently stir the tomatoes and arugula into the pasta. Serve garnished with the thyme leaves.

You can give this salad a different twist by replacing the grapes with pears—you'll soon understand why they're the traditional partner for blue cheese and walnuts.

chicken, cheese and arugula salad

serves 4

5½ ounces arugula leaves

2 celery stalks, sliced

½ cucumber, sliced

2 scallions, sliced

2 tablespoons chopped fresh flat-leaf parsley

¼ cup chopped walnuts

12 ounces cold roast chicken, sliced

4½ ounces blue cheese, cubed

Handful of seedless red grapes, cut in half (optional)

Salt and pepper

For the dressing:

2 tablespoons olive oil

1 tablespoon sherry vinegar

1 teaspoon whole grain mustard

1 tablespoon chopped fresh mixed herbs

Put the arugula leaves into a large bowl. Add the celery, cucumber, scallions, parsley, and walnuts, and mix together well. Transfer to a large serving dish.

Arrange the chicken slices over the salad, then scatter over the blue cheese. Add the grapes, if using. Season well with salt and pepper.

To make the dressing, put all the ingredients into a screw-top jar and shake well. Alternatively, put them into a bowl and mix together well. Drizzle the dressing over the salad, toss gently, and serve immediately.

This traditional pairing of chicken and almonds with spinach is given an unexpected boost with a zingy ginger and honey dressing.

chicken and spinach salad

serves 4

3 celery stalks, thinly sliced

½ cucumber, thinly sliced

2 scallions, thinly sliced

9 ounces baby spinach leaves

3 tablespoons chopped fresh flat-leaf parsley

12 ounces roast chicken, thinly sliced

Smoked almonds, to garnish

For the dressing:

1-inch piece of fresh ginger, finely grated

3 tablespoons olive oil

1 tablespoon white-wine vinegar

1 tablespoon honey

½ teaspoon ground cinnamon

Salt and pepper

Toss the celery, cucumber, and scallions in a large bowl with the spinach and parsley.

Transfer to serving plates and arrange the chicken on top of the salad.

To make the dressing, put all the ingredients into a screw-top jar and shake well. Alternatively, put them in a bowl and mix together well. Pour the dressing over the salad, garnish with a few smoked almonds and serve immediately.

Simplicity itself—succulent slices of roast chicken layered with new potatoes and crunchy fresh vegetables in a smooth, creamy dressing.

layered chicken salad

serves 4

1 pound 10 ounces new potatoes, scrubbed

1 red bell pepper, halved and seeded

1 green bell pepper, halved and seeded

2 small zucchini, sliced

1 small onion, thinly sliced

3 tomatoes, sliced

12 ounces cold roast chicken, sliced

Salt

Snipped fresh chives, to garnish

For the dressing:

2/3 cup plain yogurt

3 tablespoons mayonnaise

1 tablespoon snipped fresh chives

Salt and pepper

Put the potatoes into a large pan, add just enough cold water to cover, and bring to a boil. Reduce the heat, cover, and simmer for 15–20 minutes, until tender.

Meanwhile, preheat the broiler to high. Place the bell pepper halves, skin-side up, under the preheated broiler and cook until the skins blacken and begin to char.

Remove the bell peppers with tongs, place in a bowl, and cover with plastic wrap. Set aside until cool enough to handle, then peel off the skins and slice the flesh.

Bring a small pan of lightly salted water to a boil.

Add the zucchini, bring back to a boil, reduce the heat, and simmer for 3 minutes. Drain, rinse under cold running water, and drain again. Set aside.

To make the dressing, whisk together the yogurt, mayonnaise, and chopped chives in a small bowl until well blended. Season to taste with salt and pepper.

When the potatoes are tender, drain, cool, and slice them. Divide the potato slices equally among four plates and drizzle the dressing over them.

Top each plate with one quarter of the bell pepper and zucchini slices. Layer one quarter of the onion and tomato slices, then the sliced chicken, on top of each serving. Garnish with chopped chives and serve immediately.

chicken and spinach salad

❧

page 72

layered chicken salad

page 73

3

SOUPS AND CHILIS

This basic recipe for classic chicken broth will come in handy in so many other recipes in this cookbook.

chicken broth

makes about 2 quarts

1½ pounds chicken wings

½ pound chicken thighs, bone in

2 celery stalks, cut into large chunks

2 carrots, cut into large chunks

2 onions, cut into large chunks

1 bay leaf

8 whole black peppercorns

10 cups cold water

Place all ingredients in a large soup pot. Slowly bring to a boil. Reduce heat to low. Skim any foam that comes to the surface. Simmer very gently for 4 hours. Turn off heat, and let cool for 1 hour. Strain broth. Skim fat that comes to the surface, but leave ¼ inch, as this will seal the surface. Refrigerate, and use within 2 days, or freeze until needed.

A luxury version of a very everyday soup, this one has heavy cream and asparagus tips. You could, of course, just throw in any vegetables you find in the bottom of the refrigerator.

chicken and vegetable soup

serves 4

4 cups chicken stock

6 ounces boneless, skinless chicken breasts

Sprigs of fresh parsley and tarragon

2 garlic cloves, crushed

¾ cup baby carrots, halved

1 cup baby new potatoes, quartered

¼ cup all-purpose flour

½ cup whole milk

4–5 scallions, sliced diagonally

½ cup asparagus tips, halved and cut into 1-inch pieces

½ cup heavy cream

1 tablespoon finely chopped fresh parsley

1 tablespoon finely chopped fresh tarragon

Salt and pepper, to taste

Put the stock in a pan with the chicken, parsley and tarragon sprigs, and garlic. Bring just to a boil, then reduce the heat, cover, and simmer for 20 minutes, or until the chicken is cooked.

Remove the chicken, and strain the stock. When the chicken is cool enough to handle, cut it into bite-size pieces.

Return the stock to the pan, and bring to a gentle boil. Add the carrots, cover, and cook for 5 minutes. Add the potatoes, cover, and cook for 12 minutes, or until the vegetables are almost tender.

Meanwhile, put the flour in a small mixing bowl, and whisk in the milk to make a thick paste. Pour in a little of the stock mixture, and stir to make a smooth liquid.

Stir the flour mixture into the soup, and bring just to a boil, stirring. Boil gently for 4–5 minutes until it thickens, stirring frequently.

Add the scallions, asparagus, and chicken. Reduce the heat a little, and simmer for about 15 minutes, until all the vegetables are tender. Stir in the cream and herbs. Season, and serve.

This heartwarming soup will cure all your ills—it could be the original recipe for "chicken soup for the soul."

cream of chicken soup

serves 4

3 tablespoons unsalted butter

4 shallots, chopped

1 leek, sliced

1 pound boneless, skinless chicken breasts, chopped

2½ cups chicken stock

1 tablespoon chopped fresh parsley

1 tablespoon chopped fresh thyme, plus extra sprigs to garnish

¾ cup heavy cream

Salt and pepper

Melt the butter in a large pan over medium heat. Add the shallots and cook, stirring, for 3 minutes, until slightly softened. Add the leek and cook, stirring, for an additional 5 minutes.

Add the chicken, stock, and chopped herbs, and season to taste with salt and pepper. Bring to a boil, then reduce the heat and simmer for 25 minutes, until the chicken is tender and cooked through. Remove from the heat and let cool for 10 minutes.

Transfer the soup into a food processor or blender and process until smooth (you may need to do this in batches). Return the soup to the rinsed-out pan and warm over low heat for 5 minutes.

Stir in the cream and cook for another 2 minutes, then remove from the heat and ladle into warmed serving bowls. Garnish with thyme sprigs and serve immediately.

The fresh, light springtime colors of this soup are a tad misleading—in reality this is a heartwarming winter soup that will have the added bonus of making broccoli popular with all the family.

chicken and broccoli soup

serves 4–6

One 8-ounce head of broccoli

4 tablespoon unsalted butter

1 onion, chopped

2 tablespoons basmati rice

8 ounces boneless, skinless chicken breasts, cut into thin slivers

Scant ¼ cup whole-wheat flour

1¼ cups whole milk

2 cups chicken stock

Generous ⅓ cup corn kernels

Salt and pepper

Break the broccoli into small florets and cook in a pan of lightly salted boiling water for 3 minutes. Drain, then plunge into cold water and set aside.

Melt the butter in a pan over medium heat, add the onion, rice, and chicken, and cook, stirring frequently, for 5 minutes.

Remove the pan from the heat and stir in the flour.

Return to the heat and cook for 2 minutes, stirring constantly. Stir in the milk and then the stock. Bring to a boil, stirring constantly, then reduce the heat and let simmer for 10 minutes.

Drain the broccoli and add to the pan with the corn. Taste and adjust the seasoning, adding salt and pepper if needed. Let simmer for 5 minutes, or until the rice is tender. Ladle into warmed bowls and serve immediately.

This easy and brightly flavored soup is inspired by the Mexican classic, tortilla soup. Serve with tortilla chips, cheese and sour cream, or eat as-is for a light and tasty meal.

southwestern-style chicken soup

serves 6

1 tablespoon vegetable oil

1 large onion, chopped

½ cup chopped celery

½ cup chopped carrots

6 large cloves garlic, minced

4 boneless, skinless chicken breasts

8 cups chicken stock

One 14-ounce can crushed tomatoes in puree

2 jalapeño peppers, seeded and minced

1 teaspoon ground cumin

1 teaspoon chile powder

¼ teaspoon ground coriander

½ teaspoon salt, or to taste

1 teaspoon freshly ground black pepper

2 tablespoons chopped fresh cilantro leaves

Optional toppings: sour cream, grated cheese, and broken tortilla chips

Heat the oil in a large pot. Add the onions, celery, and carrots, and cook over medium-low heat for 8 minutes, or until the onions start to turn golden. Add the garlic, and cook for 30 seconds. Add the chicken breasts, chicken stock, tomatoes, jalapeños, cumin, chile powder, coriander, salt, pepper, and the cilantro, if using. Bring to a boil, then cook on low for 15 minutes.

Remove chicken breasts from soup with tongs, and allow them to cool on a plate. When the chicken is cool enough to handle, shred, and add back to soup. Continue simmering the soup until the vegetables are tender. Serve soup hot with broken tortilla chips and other optional toppings.

Adding chicken to this already hearty soup increases the protein content and provides a great way to use up leftover chicken meat. Just substitute for the boneless, skinless chicken breast called for.

chicken corn chowder

serves 8

3 strips bacon, diced

1 large onion, diced

1 carrots, diced

1 celery stalk, diced

1 green bell pepper, diced

1 pound red potatoes, peeled and cut into ¼-inch dice

1 pound boneless, skinless chicken breast, cut into ¼-inch cubes

6 cups chicken broth

2 fresh thyme sprigs

3 cups freshly cut or frozen corn kernels

1½ cups heavy cream

Salt and freshly ground black pepper, to taste

Cook bacon in a soup pot over moderate heat, stirring, until crisp. Transfer with a slotted spoon to paper towel–lined plate, and reserve. Add onion, carrots, celery, and bell pepper to bacon drippings and cook, stirring, until onion is translucent, about 10 minutes.

Add potatoes, chicken, broth, thyme, corn and big pinch of salt. Simmer, covered, over medium-low heat until potatoes are tender. Add cream, stir, and cook uncovered for 12 minutes. Season with salt and pepper, to taste. Serve in warm bowls with the bacon sprinkled over the top.

southwestern-style chicken soup
❖
page 84

chicken corn chowder

page 85

While it doesn't get the attention that chicken noodle or chicken and rice does, chicken and barley is a great bowl of soup in its own right.

chicken and barley soup

serves 8

2 tablespoons olive oil

1 large leek, chopped

1 cup diced carrots

1 cup diced celery

3 cups sliced button mushrooms

3 cloves garlic, minced

4 cups diced red potatoes

3 cups shredded or cubed cooked chicken

10 cups chicken broth

1 cup quick-cooking barley

1 tablespoon unsalted butter

½ bunch chopped fresh flat-leaf parsley

Salt and pepper, to taste

Heat the olive oil in a soup pot over medium heat. Cook leek, carrots, celery, mushrooms, and garlic until the onions are translucent, about 5–6 minutes. Add potatoes, chicken, and broth. Stir, and bring to a boil. Add the barley, stir, reduce heat, cover, and simmer for 25 minutes.

When barley is cooked, remove soup from heat, and stir in the butter and parsley. Season with salt and pepper, to taste. Serve immediately.

The addition of tortellini to this easy chicken soup makes for a much more substantial meal. If you prefer, you can substitute your favorite ravioli instead.

chicken and tortellini soup

serves 6

1 tablespoon olive oil

1 tablespoon unsalted butter

1 pound boneless, skinless chicken (breast or thighs), cut into small cubes

½ teaspoon dried thyme

¼ teaspoon dried rosemary

1 small onion, diced

1 cup diced carrot

1 cup diced celery

1 red bell pepper, diced

1 teaspoon salt

1 teaspoon pepper

2 cloves garlic, minced

8 cups chicken broth

½ pound frozen cheese tortellini

½ cup frozen peas

Heat the olive oil and butter in a large soup pot, over medium heat. Add the chicken, thyme, rosemary, onion, carrot, celery, red bell pepper, salt and pepper. Sauté for about 5 minutes. Add the garlic and cook for 1 minute.

Increase the temperature to medium high. Add chicken broth, and bring to a simmer. Reduce to low heat. Cook until the vegetables are almost tender, about 20 minutes. Stir in tortellini and peas. Simmer for 10 minutes, or until the tortellini is cooked. Serve immediately.

Delicious and nutritious, this chicken and wild rice soup does take a few hours to come together, but one taste and you'll agree it was worth the wait.

chicken and wild rice soup

serves 6

1 tablespoon unsalted butter

1 yellow onion, diced

½ cup diced celery

1 cup diced carrots

1 clove garlic, minced

¾ cup uncooked wild rice

½ teaspoon dried rosemary

1 bay leaf

Juice of one lemon

4 boneless, skinless chicken breasts

8 cups chicken broth

Pinch of cayenne pepper

Salt and pepper, to taste

Combine all ingredients in a soup pot. Bring to a simmer over high heat. Reduce heat to low, cover, and cook for 3 hours, stirring occasionally. Remove chicken, shred with two forks, and add back to pot. Serve immediately.

This soup is so easy and tasty that it's kind of surprising that it's not much more popular than it is. For some added kick, try adding some minced fresh jalapeño.

chicken tortilla soup

serves 4

1 tablespoon vegetable oil

1 chopped yellow onion

2 cloves garlic, minced

2 boneless, skinless chicken breasts, cut into ¼-inch cubes

6 cups chicken broth

1 cup diced tomato

Juice from 1 lemon

½ teaspoon ancho chile powder

¼ teaspoon cumin

¹/₈ teaspoon chipotle chile powder

2 tablespoon chopped cilantro

1 avocado, peeled, seeded, cubed

2 cups broken corn tortilla chips

½ cup shredded Monterey Jack cheese

Place a soup pot over medium heat, add the oil and cook the onions and garlic for 3 minutes. Add the chicken, broth, tomato, lemon, ancho chile powder, cumin, and chipotle chile powder.

Bring to a simmer, reduce heat to low, and cook for 20 minutes. Turn off heat, and stir in cilantro and avocado. Add ½ cup chips into warm bowls, and serve soup over chips. Top with Monterey Jack cheese. Serve immediately.

You know that popular book that was supposed to be like chicken soup for the soul? This is chicken soup for the soul.

mom's chicken noodle soup

serves 6

For the broth:

1 large whole chicken (about 4–5 pounds)

Salt and freshly ground black pepper, to taste

1 carrot, chopped

1 celery stalk, chopped

1 onion, chopped

1 garlic clove, peeled

4 sprigs thyme

1 bay leaf

1 whole clove

½ teaspoon ketchup

For the soup:

1 tablespoon unsalted butter

1 onion, diced

1 cup diced carrots

1 cup diced celery

¼ teaspoon poultry seasoning

2 cups uncooked egg noodles or other pasta

1 tablespoon chopped fresh flat-leaf parsley

Preheat oven to 450°F.

Season the chicken inside and out with salt and pepper. Add the carrots, celery and onions to an oiled 9x13–inch baking dish, and place the chicken on top. Roast for 60 minutes, or until a thermometer inserted in the thickest part of a thigh registers 160°F.

Remove the chicken from the oven, and allow to rest until cool enough to handle. Pull off the breast meat, and larger pieces of thigh and leg meat, and refrigerate until needed.

Transfer the chicken carcass and vegetables from the roasting pan into a large stockpot. Add 2 quarts of cold water, along with the garlic, thyme, bay leaf, clove, and ketchup. Bring to a boil, turn down heat to low, and simmer for 2 hours. The liquid level should remain about the same, so every so often add a splash of water to the pot.

While the broth is simmering, melt the butter in a soup pot over medium-low heat. Sauté the diced onion, carrots, and celery in the butter until they begin to soften, about 15 minutes. Stir in the poultry seasoning, turn off the heat, and reserve until the broth is done.

Skim the fat from the top of the broth, and strain it into the soup pot with the sautéed vegetables; bring to a boil. Turn down to low and simmer until the vegetables are tender. Taste, and add salt and freshly ground black pepper, to taste. Turn heat up to high, add the egg noodles, and boil for 7 minutes. Dice the chicken, and add to the pot. Turn heat down to medium, and simmer until the noodles are tender. Stir in the parsley, and serve.

chicken tortilla soup

page 94

mom's chicken noodle soup
❦
page 95

Is this called 5-alarm chili because its spicy kick will have alarms ringing at the local firehouse? It's great served with cornbread.

5 - alarm chicken chili

serves 6

1 tablespoon vegetable oil

1 large yellow onion, diced

2 pounds ground chicken

3 cloves garlic, minced

¼ cup ancho chile powder

1 tablespoon ground cumin

1 teaspoon freshly ground black pepper

½ teaspoon chipotle chile powder

¼ teaspoon cayenne pepper

1 teaspoon dried oregano

1 teaspoon sugar

1 large green bell pepper, seeded and diced

1 large red bell pepper, seeded and diced

One 15-ounce can tomato sauce

2 tablespoons tomato paste

3 cups water, or more as needed

One 15-ounce can pinto beans, drained, not rinsed

One 15-ounce can kidney beans, drained, not rinsed

Optional garnishes: sour cream, grated pepper jack cheese, diced onions, fresh cilantro

Add the oil and onion to a Dutch oven or other heavy pot. Place over medium-high heat and sauté for about 5 minutes, or until the onions begin to soften. Add the ground chicken, and cook for about 5 minutes. As the chicken browns, use a wooden spoon to break the meat into very small pieces.

Add the garlic, chili powder, cumin, black pepper, chipotle, cayenne, oregano, and sugar. Cook, stirring, for 2 minutes.

Stir in the bell peppers, tomato sauce, tomato paste, and water. Bring to a simmer; reduce the heat to medium-low and cook, uncovered, stirring occasionally for 60 minutes.

After 30 minutes, stir in the beans, and simmer for another 10 minutes. If needed, add more water anytime during the cooking to adjust desired thickness. Taste for salt and pepper, and adjust. Serve hot, garnished with sour cream, grated pepper jack cheese, diced onions, and fresh cilantro.

When you're in the mood for the big, bold flavors of chili but want something a little lighter, give this hearty version a try.

chicken and white-bean chili

serves 6

2 tablespoons vegetable oil

2 pounds boneless, skinless chicken thighs, cut into 1-inch pieces

1 onion, diced

3 garlic cloves, minced

1 teaspoon salt

2 tablespoons ground cumin

½ teaspoon ground chipotle chile powder

¼ teaspoon cinnamon

½ teaspoon freshly ground black pepper

1 red bell pepper, seeded, diced

1 green bell pepper, seeded, diced

1 jalapeño pepper, seeded, diced

One 10-ounce can diced tomato with green chiles

3 cups chicken broth, plus more as needed

Two 15-ounce cans cannellini beans, Great Northern, or navy beans, drained

Cayenne pepper, to taste

Chopped fresh cilantro, to garnish (optional)

Add oil to a large, heavy pot over medium-high heat. When the oil's hot, add the chunks of chicken, and sauté for 5 minutes. Add the onions, garlic, and salt, and cook, stirring, for another 2 minutes. Add the cumin, chipotle, cinnamon, and pepper. Cook, stirring, for another minute.

Add the red bell pepper, green bell pepper, jalapeño pepper, diced tomato with green chiles, and chicken broth. Bring to a simmer, turn heat to low, and cook, stirring occasionally, for 30 minutes.

Stir in the beans, and simmer another 30 minutes. Taste and adjust for salt and pepper. Serve hot with a shake of cayenne and cilantro, if desired.

If you've never cooked with tomatillos before, this delicious chicken stew recipe is a great place to start.

chile verde chicken stew

serves 4

2 tablespoons vegetable oil

Salt and freshly ground black pepper, to taste

1 whole chicken, cut up into 8 serving-size pieces

1 onion, diced

8–10 tomatillos, husk removed, quartered, about 3 cups (may substitute canned)

2 jalapeños, seeded, chopped

6 cloves garlic, peeled

½ bunch cilantro, leaves picked from stems

3 cups chicken stock

2 tablespoons ground cumin

2 teaspoons dried oregano

1 bay leaf

1½ pounds potatoes, cut into large chunks

Sour cream (optional), for serving

Add oil to a Dutch oven, and place over medium-high heat. Season the chicken with salt and freshly ground black pepper, and brown well in the hot oil. Remove chicken, reduce the heat to medium, and add the onions. Sauté for about 5 minutes to soften.

While the onions are cooking, add tomatillos, jalapeños, garlic, cilantro, and chicken stock to a blender and puree until smooth. Add the chicken back to the pot, pour over the tomatillo mixture, and stir in cumin, oregano, and bay leaf. Bring to simmer, reduce heat to medium-low, cover, and simmer for 40 minutes, stirring occasionally.

Add the potato, pushing the chunks under the liquid so that they cook evenly. Cover and cook for another 30 minutes, or until the potatoes are tender. Serve hot in bowls with a dollop of sour cream.

Soup has a very important place in Thai cuisine—try this fragrant, delicately flavored offering and you'll soon see why!

thai chicken soup

serves 6

1 tablespoon sesame oil or chili oil

2 garlic cloves, chopped

2 scallions, sliced

1 leek, finely sliced

1 tablespoon grated fresh ginger

1 red chile, seeded and finely chopped

12 ounces boneless, skinless chicken breasts, cut into strips

Scant 3½ cups chicken stock

2 tablespoons rice wine

1 tablespoon chopped lemongrass

6 kaffir lime leaves, finely shredded

7 ounces fine egg noodles

Salt and pepper

Heat the oil in a wok or large pan. Add the garlic and cook over medium heat, stirring, for 1 minute. Add the scallions, leek, ginger, and chile, and cook, stirring, for an additional 3 minutes.

Add the chicken, stock, and rice wine, bring to a boil, reduce the heat, and simmer for 20 minutes. Stir in the lemongrass and lime leaves.

Bring a separate pan of water to a boil and add the noodles. Cook for 3 minutes, or according to the package instructions, then drain well and add to the soup. Season to taste with salt and pepper. Cook for another 2 minutes. Remove from the heat, ladle into warmed serving bowls, and serve immediately.

PAN-FRIED CHICKEN

Chicken fajitas are a great choice when you want delicious but healthy Mexican food.
This marinade works on pork and steak, too.

chicken fajitas

serves 4

1 tablespoon ground cumin

1 tablespoon ancho chile powder

Salt and pepper, to taste

Juice and zest from 1 lime

4 boneless, skinless chicken breasts, sliced into thin strips

2 tablespoons vegetable oil

2 bell peppers, sliced thin

1 onion, sliced thin

8 flour tortillas

1 avocado, sliced, for serving

½ cup cilantro, coarsely chopped, for serving

½ cup sour cream, for serving

½ cup shredded Monterey Jack cheese, for serving

Jarred salsa (optional), for serving

Mix the cumin, chile powder, salt, pepper, lime zest and juice. Place chicken in a sealable plastic bag and pour the marinade in. Massage with your hands so each piece is coated with the marinade. Seal and marinate for 2 hours. Remove chicken from marinade, and pat dry with paper towels.

Heat 1 tablespoon of the oil in a cast-iron or heavy skillet over high heat. Sear the chicken in batches, until browned, and cooked through. Reserve on a plate.

Heat remaining oil in the same pan over medium-high heat. Add the bell peppers and onions and cook, stirring, occasionally, 5–6 minutes, until firm but tender.

Warm the tortillas under a broiler for a minute or two. Serve the chicken, peppers and onions on warm tortillas. Garnish with avocado, cilantro, sour cream, cheese, and salsa.

Chicken piccata is a popular item in Italian-American restaurants, and consists of chicken-breast medallions in a delicious lemon and caper sauce.

chicken piccata

serves 4

4 boneless, skinless chicken breasts, pounded to ¼-inch thickness

Salt and freshly ground black pepper, as needed

All-purpose flour, for dredging

¼ cup olive oil

2 tablespoons capers, drained (mince 2 teaspoons, leave the rest whole)

²/₃ cup white wine

¹/₃ cup lemon juice

¹/₃ cup chicken broth or water

6 tablespoons cold unsalted butter, cut in ¼-inch slices

¼ cup fresh flat-leaf parsley, chopped

Season chicken breasts with salt and pepper. Dredge chicken in the flour until completely covered. Shake off excess, and reserve.

Add the olive oil to large skillet and place over medium-high heat. When the oil is hot, add chicken and cook for about 4 minutes per side, or until browned and just cooked through. Remove to a plate, cover loosely with foil, and reserve.

Add the capers and wine to the skillet. Turn heat up to high, and boil until the wine has reduced by about half. Use a spatula to scrape the caramelized bits from the bottom of the pan.

Add the lemon juice and chicken broth, and bring to a boil. Cook for 2 minutes, reduce heat to low, and add chicken back into the pan. Cook the chicken in the sauce until heated through.

Place chicken on a serving platter. Add the butter and parsley to the skillet, and whisk until the butter emulsifies into the sauce. Check the seasoning, and spoon the hot sauce over the chicken; serve immediately.

chicken fajitas

❖

page 108

chicken piccata

page 109

Italian cooks often use Marsala wine to add depth of flavor and bring out the best when cooking white meat, such as the chicken in this impressive dinner dish.

chicken and mushroom marsala

serves 4

4 thick slices Italian or French bread

2 tablespoon olive oil, plus extra for brushing

1 whole garlic clove

4 large boneless chicken breasts, skin on

Salt and pepper

8 large white mushrooms, sliced

2 tablespoons finely minced shallot

2 garlic cloves, minced fine

1½ tablespoons all-purpose flour

1½ cup Marsala wine

2 cups chicken stock

1 tablespoon freshly chopped flat-leaf parsley

2 tablespoons cold unsalted butter, cut in small pieces

Salt and pepper

Preheat the broiler. Lightly brush the bread slices with olive oil, and toast under the broiler until golden brown on both sides. Rub the whole garlic clove thoroughly over the toasted surface of each slice. Set aside until needed.

Season the chicken breasts on both sides generously with salt and pepper. Heat the olive oil in a large skillet over medium-high heat. Place the chicken skin-side down and sear for 5 minutes. Turn over and cook for another 5 minutes, or until the chicken is tender and the juices run clear when a sharp knife is inserted into the thickest part of the meat. Remove from the skillet and set aside.

Add the mushrooms and a pinch of salt to the pan, reduce the heat to medium and cook the mushrooms until they begin to soften and give up their juices. Continue cooking until the liquid evaporates and the mushrooms begin to brown. Add the shallots and garlic and cook, stirring, for 1 minute. Add the flour and cook, stirring, for an additional 2 minutes.

Carefully add the Marsala, turn up the heat to high, and cook, stirring, for 2 minutes. While it cooks, scrape the bottom of the pan with a whisk to deglaze any of the caramelized bits. Add the chicken stock and boil until the sauce begins to reduce and thicken slightly.

Reduce the heat to very low, return the chicken breasts to the pan and reheat gently. Place a garlic toast on each of four serving plates and top with a chicken breast. Whisk the parsley and butter into the sauce, then spoon the sauce over the top and serve immediately.

Tangy goat cheese really turns this mushroom cream sauce into something extraordinary.

chicken cutlets with creamy goat cheese-mushroom sauce

serves 4

4 boneless, skinless chicken breasts, halved, pounded to eight ¼-inch thick cutlets

Salt and freshly ground black pepper, to taste

2 tablespoons olive oil

¼ pound sliced mushrooms

1 tablespoon unsalted butter

¼ cup chicken broth

½ cup heavy cream

3 ounces goat cheese

¼ cup chopped flat-leaf parsley

Season the chicken with salt and freshly ground black pepper. Heat oil in a large skillet over medium-high heat. Cook the chicken about 3 minutes per side, or until browned and cooked through. Transfer to a plate.

Add the mushrooms and butter to the pan and cook, stirring occasionally, until liquid has evaporated, and the mushrooms have browned. Stir in the broth, heavy cream, goat cheese, and parsley. Bring to a simmer, add the chicken, and cook until the cutlets are heated through. Season with salt and freshly ground black pepper, to taste, if needed. Serve immediately.

It doesn't get much easier than this. This simple recipe is great for a quick meal or a fancy dinner party. You can also use any type of mustard you like.

chicken with stone-ground mustard cream sauce

serves 4

1 tablespoon unsalted butter

1 tablespoon olive oil

4 boneless, skinless chicken breasts, pounded to ½-inch thickness

Salt and pepper, to taste

½ cup chicken broth

⅔ cup heavy cream

2 tablespoons stone-ground mustard

2 tablespoons chopped fresh flat-leaf parsley

Add butter and oil to a large skillet over medium high heat. Season the chicken breasts generously with salt and pepper. Sauté about 5 minutes per side until cooked through. Remove to a plate, and cover with foil.

Add the chicken broth into the pan. Whisk in the cream, mustard, and parsley. Cook for about 3 minutes, until sauce thickened. Pour the sauce over the chicken, and serve.

Not what you might expect—the peas used in this recipe are not the garden variety but nutty black-eyed peas, combined with delicious smoky Asian spices.

chicken with peas

serves 4

1 cup dried black-eyed peas, soaked overnight and drained

1 teaspoon salt

2 onions, finely chopped

2 garlic cloves, minced

1 teaspoon ground turmeric

1 teaspoon ground cumin

1 whole chicken (about 3 pounds) cut into 8 pieces

1 green bell pepper, seeded and chopped

2 tablespoons olive oil

1-inch piece of fresh ginger, grated

2 teaspoons coriander seeds

½ teaspoon fennel seeds

1 tablespoon chopped fresh cilantro, for garnish

Put the black-eyed peas into a large pan with the salt, onions, garlic, turmeric, and cumin. Cover the peas with water, bring to a boil, and cook for 15 minutes.

Add the chicken and bell pepper to the pan with the peas and return to a boi, and bring to a boil. Reduce the heat, and let simmer for 30 minutes until the peas are tender and the chicken juices run clear when the thickest parts of the pieces are pierced with the point of a sharp knife.

Heat the oil in a wok or skillet, and stir-fry the ginger, coriander seeds, and fennel seeds for 30 seconds.

Stir the fried spices into the chicken. Let simmer for an additional 5 minutes, garnish with the chopped cilantro, and serve immediately.

With its lovely warm, vibrant orange color, this family dinner dish will certainly light up your life.

sunshine chicken

serves 4

1 pound boneless, skinless chicken breasts

1½ tablespoons all-purpose flour

Salt and freshly ground pepper, to taste

1 tablespoon olive oil

1 onion, cut into wedges

2 celery stalks, sliced

⅔ cup orange juice

1¼ cups chicken broth

1 tablespoon light soy sauce

1–2 teaspoons honey

1 tablespoon grated orange zest

1 orange bell pepper, seeded and chopped

1–2 zucchini, sliced into semicircles

2 small corn cobs, halved, or ½ cup corn kernels

1 orange, peeled and segmented

1 tablespoon chopped fresh parsley, to garnish

Lightly rinse the chicken and pat dry with paper towels. Cut into bite-size pieces. Season the flour well with salt and pepper. Toss the chicken in the seasoned flour until well coated and reserve any remaining seasoned flour.

Heat the oil in a large, heavy-bottom skillet and cook the chicken over high heat, stirring frequently, for 5 minutes, or until golden on all sides and browned. Using a slotted spoon, transfer to a plate.

Add the onion and celery to the skillet and cook over medium heat, stirring frequently, for 5 minutes, or until softened. Sprinkle in the reserved seasoned flour and cook, stirring constantly, for 2 minutes, then remove from the heat. Gradually stir in the orange juice, broth, soy sauce, and honey, followed by the orange zest, then return to the heat and bring to a boil, stirring.

Return the chicken to the skillet. Reduce the heat, then cover and simmer, stirring occasionally, for 15 minutes. Add the orange bell pepper, zucchini, and corn and simmer for an additional 10 minutes, or until the chicken and vegetables are tender. Add the orange segments, then stir well and heat through for 1 minute. Serve garnished with the parsley.

This is such an old favorite— just one taste of this delicious classic dish and you'll understand why.

chicken in red wine (coq au vin)

serves 4

4 tablespoons unsalted butter

2 tablespoons olive oil

4 pounds chicken pieces

4 ounces smoked bacon, cut into strips

½ cup pearl onions, peeled

½ cup cremini mushrooms, halved

2 garlic cloves, finely chopped

2 tablespoons brandy

1 cup red wine

1¼ cups chicken stock

1 tablespoon mixed herbs

Salt and pepper, to taste

2 tablespoons all-purpose flour

Bay leaves, to garnish

Melt 2 tablespoons of the butter with the olive oil in a large, dutch oven or heavy skillet. Add the chicken, and cook over medium heat, turning occasionally, for 8–10 minutes, or until golden-brown. Add the bacon, onions, mushrooms, and garlic.

Pour in the brandy, and set it alight with a match or lighter. When the flames have died down, add the wine, stock, and mixed herbs, and season to taste with salt and pepper. Bring to a boil, reduce the heat, and simmer gently for 1 hour, or until the chicken pieces are cooked through and tender.

Meanwhile, create the thickener for the sauce by blending the remaining butter with the flour in a small bowl.

Transfer the chicken to a large plate and keep warm. Stir the butter and flour mixture into the pan sauce a little at a time. Bring to a boil, return the chicken to the casserole, and serve immediately, garnished with bay leaves.

The sweetness of port wine makes for a great pan sauce to spoon over these pan-seared chicken breasts. If you don't have port wine, try sherry.

chicken breasts with port-wine sauce

serves 4

4 boneless chicken breasts, skin on

Salt and freshly ground black pepper, to taste

2 tablespoons olive oil

1 shallot, finely minced

1 clove garlic, minced

1 tablespoon all-purpose flour

1 cup port wine

1½ cups chicken stock

1 tablespoons fresh flat-leaf parsley, chopped

2 tablespoons cold unsalted butter, cut into small pieces

Season chicken breasts on both sides. Heat the olive oil in a large skillet over medium-high heat until hot. Place the chicken skin-side down and sear for 5 minutes. Turn over and cook for another 5 minutes, or until just cooked through. Transfer to a plate and reserve while you make the sauce.

Add the shallot and pinch of salt to the hot pan, reduce the heat to medium-low, and add the garlic and flour. Cook, stirring, for 3 minutes. Carefully add the port, turn heat to high, and cook, stirring, for 2 minutes. Add the chicken stock and cook until the sauce begins to reduce and thicken, about 3–4 minutes.

Reduce the heat to low, and add the chicken breasts back into the pan. Toss in the sauce to coat and reheat the chicken for a few minutes. Turn off the heat, and plate each chicken breast. Add the parsley and butter to the sauce, and whisk until butter disappears. Adjust seasoning with salt and freshly ground black pepper, spoon the sauce over the top of the chicken, and serve immediately.

This chicken breast is very light, but not lacking in taste. The flavorful poaching liquid gently cooks the breasts and then reduces to make an easy sauce

lemon and tarragon-poached chicken breast

serves 4

1 cup white wine

2 cups chicken broth

1 bunch tarragon, leaves picked

½ onion, sliced

½ teaspoon salt

Pinch of freshly ground black pepper

Pinch of cayenne pepper

Juice of 1 lemon

4 boneless, skinless chicken breasts

1 tablespoon cold unsalted butter

Lemon wedges, to garnish

2 cups cooked mashed potatoes (optional)

Add the wine, chicken broth, tarragon, onion, salt, black pepper, cayenne, and lemon juice to a 10-inch skillet (pan should be just large enough to fit the 4 chicken breasts). Bring to a simmer over high heat, and add chicken breasts. Turn the heat down to very low, and simmer the chicken breasts gently for 12 minutes, or until internal temperature of 160–165°F.

Transfer the breasts to a plate, and cover with foil. Turn the heat up to high and boil the liquid for 5 minutes to reduce. Turn off heat, toss in the cold butter, and whisk until dissolved. Taste for salt, and adjust seasoning.

Place a scoop of mashed potatoes into four warm bowls. Slice the breasts, and arrange over the potatoes. Spoon over the hot sauce. Serve immediately with extra lemon wedges, if desired.

This truckstop special features pan-fried chicken breasts covered in a simple but savory onion gravy. It's great over rice, which soaks up the sauce.

smothered chicken breasts

serves 4

4 bone-in chicken breasts, skin on

1 teaspoon poultry seasoning

Salt and freshly ground black pepper, to taste

2 tablespoon vegetable oil

1 tablespoon unsalted butter

1 large yellow onion, sliced

4 cloves garlic, finely minced

1 rounded tablespoon all-purpose flour

1½ cup chicken broth

¼ cup buttermilk

¼ cup water

4 cups cooked rice (optional)

Season chicken breasts on both sides with the poultry seasoning, salt, and pepper. Heat the oil in a large skillet over medium-high heat. When the oil is hot, brown the chicken breasts skin-side down, about 4 minutes per side. Remove from the pan, and reserve on a plate.

Pour off the excess oil, and place the pan back on the stove over medium heat. Add the butter and the onions, along with a big pinch of salt. Sauté for about 10 minutes, or until the onions are well browned. The onions need to caramelize for best results.

Stir in the garlic, and cook for 1 minute. Stir in the flour, and cook for 2 minutes. Add the chicken broth, buttermilk, and water. As the mixture comes to a simmer, use a wooden spoon to scrape any browned bits from the bottom of the pan.

Turn the heat to low, and let the onion gravy gently simmer for 15 minutes. Add a splash of water if it seems to be getting too thick. Add the chicken breasts and any juices back into the pan, and coat with the gravy. Cover, and cook for about 20 minutes, or until the chicken is cooked through. Taste for seasoning, and adjust if needed. Serve chicken breasts over rice, topped with the onion gravy.

Chives are a sort of cross between shallots and onions and make for a great accompaniment for this chicken recipe.

chicken with creamed shallots

serves 4

1 whole chicken, cut into quarters Kosher salt, as needed

Freshly ground black pepper

1 tablespoon unsalted butter

1 tablespoon olive oil

½ pound shallots, peeled, cut in thick ½-inch-wide slices

2 tablespoons all-purpose flour

½ cup white wine

1 cup chicken broth

¼ cup cream

1 tablespoon freshly chopped chives

Season chicken generously with salt and pepper on both sides. Heat the butter and oil in Dutch oven over medium-high heat. Sear the chicken in the fat, about 4 minutes on each side. Transfer chicken to a plate, and add the shallots to the Dutch oven. Lower heat and cook for 5 minutes, or until golden. Add the flour, and stir in. Cook for 2 minutes.

Add the wine and chicken broth, and bring to a boil, scraping any browned bits from the bottom. Return the chicken to the pot. Cover tightly, and simmer on low heat for about 40 minutes, until chicken is cooked through.

Transfer the chicken to a platter, and cover loosely with foil. Turn heat to high, add the cream, bring to a boil, and cook for 5 minutes, or until reduced and slightly thickened. Add chives and salt and pepper, to taste. Pour the sauce over chicken, and serve immediately.

smothered chicken breasts

page 126

chicken with creamed shallots

❖

page 127

Pomegranate juice was once a rare and exotic treat, but now you can find it in practically every store. It makes for a wonderfully different braised-chicken dish.

pomegranate chicken

serves 6

2 teaspoons olive oil

2 pounds boneless, skinless chicken thighs

Salt and pepper, to taste

1 medium onion, chopped

2 cloves minced garlic

2 teaspoons ground cumin

1 teaspoon cinnamon

½ teaspoon turmeric

1¼ cup pomegranate juice

1 cup chicken broth

2 tablespoons chopped fresh flat-leaf parsley

Heat oil in a large skillet. Season chicken with salt and pepper to taste, and sear thighs over medium-high heat on both sides and transfer to a plate. Add onions to the skillet, and cook until softened, about 5 minutes. Add the rest of the ingredients along with the reserved chicken.

Cook uncovered for about 30 minutes, or until chicken is cooked and sauce has reduced and thickened slightly.

This Chinese-American take-out favorite is fairly easy to make at home and probably far lower in fat and calories than the restaurant version.

general tso's chicken

serves 2–3

For the sauce:

¼ cup water

3 tablespoons rice vinegar

3 tablespoons soy sauce

1 tablespoon hoisin sauce

2 tablespoons sugar

½ tablespoon dry sherry wine

2 teaspoons cornstarch

For the chicken:

1 pound bite-sized pieces (about 1-inch) boneless, skinless chicken meat (thighs or breasts)

½ tablespoon dry sherry wine

¼ teaspoon salt

¼ cup cornstarch

Vegetable oil for deep-frying

2 tablespoons vegetable oil for sautéing

1 tablespoon finely minced ginger

2 cloves garlic, finely minced

1 teaspoon red chile flakes

3 green onions, white parts only, chopped

Mix all the ingredients for the sauce in a small mixing bowl, and set aside.

Marinate the chicken meat with the sherry wine and salt for 10 minutes. Coat the chicken with the cornstarch. Heat oil for deep-frying to 350°F. Fry the chicken about 5 minutes, until browned and cooked through. Remove with a strainer, draining the excess oil on a plate lined with paper towels.

Heat a large skillet over high heat and add the 2 tablespoons oil. Add the ginger, garlic, and red chile flakes, stir-fry for 1 minute. Pour the sauce into the pan. Bring sauce to a boil, and when it thickens, add the chicken, and toss to combine with the sauce. Stir in the onions, and serve immediately.

This may be the most famous garlic-chicken recipe ever. You don't need to count the cloves, but we all know you're going to.

chicken with forty cloves of garlic

serves 4

3 whole heads garlic, separated into about 40 cloves

1 whole chicken, cut into quarters

Kosher salt, as needed

Freshly ground black pepper

1 tablespoon unsalted butter

1 tablespoon olive oil

1 cup white wine

½ cup chicken broth

1 tablespoon fresh picked thyme leaves

2 tablespoons all-purpose flour

2 tablespoons heavy cream

¼ cup water

Prep garlic cloves by blanching them in boiling water for 1 minute, draining, and peeling when cooled. Reserve until needed.

Season chicken generously with salt and pepper on both sides. Heat the butter and oil in Dutch oven over medium-high heat. Sear the chicken in the fat, about 4 minutes on each side. Remove chicken to a plate, and add all of the garlic to the pot. Lower heat and cook for 10 minutes, or until golden-brown.

Add the wine and chicken broth, and bring to a boil, scraping any browned bits from the bottom. Return the chicken to the pot and add the thyme leaves. Cover tightly and simmer on low heat for about 40 minutes, until chicken is cooked through.

Remove the chicken to a platter and cover loosely with foil. In a bowl, whisk together ½ cup of pan drippings with the flour, and then whisk it back into the rest of the sauce in the pot. Turn heat to medium-high, add the cream and water, bring to a simmer, and cook for 5 minutes. Add salt and pepper, to taste. Pour the sauce and garlic cloves over chicken, and serve immediately.

Whoever said chicken was boring could never have had the pleasure of tasting this dish—so hot it almost dances right off the plate and into your mouth!

red-hot chile chicken

serves 4

For the chile paste:

1 tablespoon curry paste

2 fresh green chiles, chopped

5 dried red chiles

2 tablespoons tomato paste

2 garlic cloves, chopped

1 teaspoon chile powder

Pinch of sugar

Pinch of salt

2 tablespoons vegetable oil

½ teaspoon cumin seeds

1 onion, chopped

2 curry leaves

1 teaspoon ground cumin

1 teaspoon ground coriander

½ teaspoon ground turmeric

One 14.5-ounce can chopped tomatoes

²⁄₃ cup chicken stock

4 6-ounce boneless, skinless chicken breasts

4 cups freshly cooked rice, to serve

Fresh mint sprigs, to garnish

To make the chile paste, place the curry paste, fresh and dried chiles, tomato paste, garlic, chili powder, sugar, and salt in a blender or food processor, and process to a smooth paste.

Heat the oil in a large, heavy-bottomed pan. Add the cumin seeds and cook over medium heat, stirring constantly, for 2 minutes, or until they begin to pop and release their aroma. Add the onion and curry leaves and cook, stirring, for 5 minutes.

Add the chili paste, cook for 2 minutes, then stir in the ground cumin, coriander, and turmeric and cook for an additional 2 minutes.

Add the tomatoes and their juices, and the stock. Bring to a boil, then reduce the heat and simmer for 5 minutes. Add the chicken, cover, and simmer gently for 20 minutes, or until the chicken is cooked through and tender.

Serve immediately with the rice and garnished with fresh mint sprigs.

Garlic and chicken—perfect partners. Citrus fruit and chicken—simply a great match. Put them together and you get an irresistible flavor sensation. Enjoy!

garlic and lime chicken

serves 4

Four 6-ounce boneless, skinless chicken breasts

For the garlic butter:
3 tablespoons softened unsalted butter
2 cloves garlic, finely chopped

3 tablespoons chopped fresh cilantro
1 tablespoon vegetable oil
Finely grated zest and juice of 2 limes, plus extra zest, for garnish
¼ cup firmly packed brown sugar
Boiled rice and lemon wedges, for serving

Place each chicken breast between 2 sheets of plastic wrap and pound with a rolling pin until flattened to about ½-inch thick.

To make the garlic butter: Mix the softened butter with the garlic.

Mix together the garlic butter and cilantro and spread over each flattened chicken breast. Roll up like a jelly roll and secure with a toothpick.

Heat the oil in a preheated wok or heavy bottom skillet. Add the chicken rolls to the wok and cook, turning, for 15–20 minutes or until cooked through.

Remove the chicken from the wok and transfer to a board. Cut each chicken roll into slices.

Add the lime zest and juice and sugar to the wok and heat gently, stirring until the sugar has dissolved. Raise the heat and allow to bubble for 2 minutes.

Arrange the chicken on warmed serving plates and spoon over the sauce to serve.

Garnish with extra lime zest, if desired, and serve with the boiled rice and lemon wedges.

Tarragon and chicken are great together, and that's certainly the case here. You can eat these patties as-is, or throw them on some buns for a great sandwich.

chicken patties with creamy tarragon sauce

makes 6 chicken patties

For the tarragon sauce:

½ teaspoon Dijon mustard

2 tablespoon mayonnaise

2 tablespoon sour cream

2 teaspoon fresh tarragon, very finely chopped

1 teaspoon lemon juice

Pinch of cayenne pepper

Pinch of salt

For the patties:

1 pound ground chicken

¹/₃ cup plain dry breadcrumbs, plus more as needed

1 large egg, beaten

1 tablespoon mayonnaise

1 tablespoon capers, chopped

1 tablespoon fresh lemon juice

1 clove garlic, crushed, finely minced

1 teaspoon fresh tarragon, finely chopped

½ teaspoon Dijon mustard

½ teaspoon salt

¼ teaspoon black pepper

2 tablespoon olive oil

1 tablespoon unsalted butter

Fresh lemon wedges, to garnish

Combine all the sauce ingredients in a small bowl, and whisk to combine. Refrigerate until needed.

Add the chicken to a mixing bowl, along with ⅓ cup breadcrumbs and the rest of the ingredients, except the oil and butter. Mix with a fork until thoroughly combined. Refrigerate for 30 minutes.

Shape chicken mixture into 6 patties about 1-inch thick, and place on a plate lightly dusted with breadcrumbs. Lightly dust the tops of the chicken patties with more breadcrumbs. Heat the oil and butter in a large skillet over medium heat until the butter melts. Cook patties for about 5 minutes per side, or until golden-brown and cooked through. Serve hot with the sauce and fresh lemon.

This great dish from South Carolina's "Low Country" is usually done with shrimp, but it's also fantastic with chicken. You can use any cut of boneless, skinless chicken.

chicken and grits

serves 4

4 strips bacon, cut in ¼-inch pieces

For the grits:

4 cups water

2 tablespoons unsalted butter

1 teaspoon salt

1 cup white grits

½ cup grated white Cheddar cheese

For the chicken:

⅓ cup water or chicken stock

2 tablespoons heavy cream

2 teaspoons lemon juice

Dash of Worcestershire sauce

3 large boneless, skinless chicken breasts, cut into 1-inch cubes

½ teaspoon Cajun seasoning

¼ teaspoon salt

¼ teaspoon black pepper

Pinch of cayenne pepper

3 cloves garlic, minced fine

2 tablespoons minced green onions

1 tablespoon minced jalapeño

1 tablespoon chopped fresh flat-leaf parsley

Cook the bacon in a large skillet over medium heat until almost crisp. Turn off the heat. Remove the bacon with a slotted spoon and reserve. Leave about 1 tablespoon of bacon fat in the pan; set aside.

To cook the grits: In a medium saucepan, bring the water, butter, and salt to a boil. Whisk in the grits, and reduce heat to low. Cook, stirring occasionally, until smooth and creamy, about 20 minutes. Turn off the heat and stir in the cheese. Cover and reserve until the chicken is done.

To cook the chicken: Mix the water, cream, lemon juice, and Worcestershire sauce in a small bowl and set aside. Combine the chicken, Cajun seasoning, salt, black pepper, and cayenne in a mixing bowl. Toss with a spatula until the chicken is coated evenly with the seasonings.

Turn the heat back on high under the skillet. When you see the first wisp of smoke, quickly add the chicken mixture. Use tongs to distribute the chicken into a single layer. Turn the heat down medium-high and cook, stirring for 5 minutes. Add the garlic, green onions, jalapeño, and reserved bacon, cook stirring for 5 minutes more. Add the liquid mixture and cook, stirring, until the chicken is cooked through. Turn off the heat, and stir in the parsley. Spoon the cheesy grits into bowls, and top with the chicken.

A simple chicken dish that is a perfect solution for a mid-week supper.

pan-fried chicken with tomato-and-bacon sauce

serves 4

For the tomato-and-bacon sauce:

2 tablespoons unsalted butter

2 tablespoons olive oil

1 large onion, finely chopped

2 garlic cloves, finely chopped

1 celery stalk, finely chopped

4 slices bacon, chopped

One 14-ounce can chopped tomatoes

2 tablespoons tomato paste

Pinch of brown sugar, to taste

½ cup water

Salt and pepper, to taste

1 tablespoon chopped fresh basil

1 tablespoon chopped fresh flat-leaf parsley, plus extra to garnish

2 tablespoons unsalted butter

2 tablespoons olive oil

4 boneless, skinless chicken breasts or
8 boneless, skinless chicken thighs

First, make the sauce. Melt the butter with the oil in a large pan. Add the onion, garlic, celery, and bacon, and cook over low heat, stirring occasionally, for 5 minutes, until softened. Stir in the tomatoes, tomato paste, sugar to taste, and water, and season with salt and pepper. Increase the heat to medium and bring to a boil, then reduce the heat and simmer, stirring occasionally, for 15–20 minutes, until thickened.

Meanwhile, melt the butter with the oil in a large skillet. Add the chicken, and cook over medium-high heat for 4–5 minutes on each side, until evenly browned.

Stir the basil and parsley into the sauce. Add the chicken, and spoon the sauce over it. Cover and simmer for 10–15 minutes, until cooked through and tender. Garnish with parsley, and serve immediately.

This perfect dish from the Deep South is best served with a bowl of steaming rice.

louisiana chicken

serves 4–6

5 tablespoons corn oil

4 chicken pieces

6 tablespoons all-purpose flour

1 onion, chopped

2 celery stalks, sliced

1 green bell pepper, seeded and chopped

2 garlic cloves, finely chopped

2 teaspoons chopped fresh thyme

2 fresh red chiles, seeded and finely chopped

One 15-ounce can chopped tomatoes

1¼ cups chicken stock

Salt and pepper, to taste

Lamb's lettuce and chopped fresh thyme, to garnish

Heat the oil in a large, heavy-bottom saucepan or Dutch oven. Add the chicken, and cook over medium heat, turning occasionally, for 5–10 minutes, or until golden. Transfer the chicken to a plate with a slotted spoon.

Stir the flour into the oil and cook over very low heat, stirring constantly, for 15 minutes, or until light-golden. Do not let it burn. Immediately add the onion, celery, and green bell pepper and cook, stirring constantly, for 2 minutes. Add the garlic, thyme, and chiles and cook, stirring, for 1 minute.

Stir in the tomatoes and their juices, and then gradually stir in the stock. Return the chicken pieces to the pan, cover, and simmer for 45 minutes, or until the chicken is cooked through and tender. Season to taste with salt and pepper, transfer to warmed serving plates, and serve immediately, garnished with some lamb's lettuce and a sprinkling of chopped thyme.

CHICKEN IN A NEST

This quick and easy casserole is a real crowd-pleaser, and perfect for feeding large groups of hungry guests.

chicken tetrazzini casserole

serves 8

1 pound spaghetti, cooked, drained, rinsed

6 boneless, skinless chicken breasts, cut into ½-inch cubes

One 10.75-ounce can condensed cream of chicken soup

One 10.75-ounce can condensed cream of mushroom soup

3 cups chicken broth

2 tablespoons chopped chives

2 tablespoons unsalted butter

½ cup shredded white Cheddar cheese

Preheat oven to 350°F.

Put cooked spaghetti into buttered 9x13-inch baking dish. In a large saucepan, mix together the chicken, soups, broth, chives, and butter. Place over medium-high heat, and bring to a simmer, stirring occasionally. Pour over the spaghetti, and mix well to combine. Pat down with a spatula. Sprinkle cheese over top. Bake at 350°F for 30 minutes, or until browned and bubbling.

Baked ziti is a classic casserole, and usually made with ground beef. This version uses ground chicken and is every bit as delicious.

baked chicken ziti

serves 8

1 yellow onion, diced

2 tablespoons olive oil

1 pound ground chicken

Two 26-ounce jars prepared pasta sauce

1 pound dry ziti pasta

1½ cups heavy cream

8 ounces sliced or shredded provolone cheese

8 ounces shredded mozzarella cheese

¼ cup grated Parmesan cheese

In a large skillet, sweat onions in the olive oil over medium heat until translucent. Add the chicken and cook for 5 minutes, breaking up the meat as it cooks. Add the sauce and simmer 20 minutes.

Cook pasta according to package directions. Drain and transfer to a large mixing bowl. Add the sauce mixture and cream, and mix to combine. Oil a large casserole dish, and add ⅓ of the pasta mixture. Scatter over half the provolone and mozzarella cheese. Add another ⅓ of the pasta, then the rest of the provolone and mozzarella cheese. Finish with the rest of the pasta. Top with Parmesan. Bake at 350°F for 40 minutes, or until bubbling and golden-brown.

chicken tetrazzini casserole

❖

page 148

baked chicken ziti

❖

page 149

Rumor has it, Chicken à la King was created in the 1890s by chef William King of the Bellevue Hotel in Philadelphia, although many others claim to be the inventor. Regardless of who invented it, it's a delicious American classic.

chicken à la king

serves 4

6 tablespoons unsalted butter

1 small onion, minced

6 tablespoons all-purpose flour

¼ cup dry sherry wine

4 cups chicken broth

1½ pounds boneless, skinless chicken thighs, cut into 1-inch pieces

1 red bell pepper, diced

1 tablespoon minced fresh flat-leaf parsley

¼ teaspoon dried thyme

Pinch of cayenne pepper

½ pound button mushrooms, cut into ½-inch slices

½ cup heavy cream

Salt and pepper, to taste

4 servings prepared buttered noodles

In a saucepan over medium heat, melt 3 tablespoons butter and sauté the onions until translucent, about 5 minutes. Add the flour, and cook, stirring, for 3 minutes. Slowly whisk in sherry and broth and bring to a boil while stirring. Add the chicken, peppers, parsley and thyme; reduce heat to low and simmer for 30 minutes, stirring occasionally.

While chicken is simmering in the sauce, heat the remaining butter in a skillet over medium-high heat. Add mushrooms and sauté until golden-brown. Add to the sauce. Whisk in the cream. When heated through, season with salt and pepper, to taste. Serve immediately over noodles.

This gumbo is a spicy, meaty, comforting Cajun stew served with rice. Andouille sausage is traditional, but any spicy sausage will work in this American classic.

chicken and sausage gumbo

serves 6

¹/₃ cup vegetable oil

¹/₃ cup all-purpose flour

1 onion, diced

2 stalks celery, diced

1 green bell pepper, diced

8 ounces Andouille sausage, or other spicy smoked sausage sliced into ¹/₂-inch thick rounds

3 cloves garlic, crushed fine

1 teaspoon salt

1¹/₂ tablespoons paprika

¹/₂ teaspoon cayenne pepper, or to taste

¹/₂ teaspoon black pepper

3 cups chicken broth, or more as needed

8 boneless, skinless chicken thighs, cut into 2-inch pieces

¹/₂ cup minced green onions

6 cups cooked rice (optional), for serving

To make the roux: In a heavy pot, cook the oil and flour over low heat, stirring, until it is a nutty, golden-brown color. This will take about 30 minutes.

Add the onion, celery, bell pepper, and salt, and cook for another 10 minutes to soften the vegetables. Add the sausage and garlic; stir and cook for 1 minute. Stir in the paprika, cayenne pepper, and black pepper. Add the broth, and turn heat up to medium-low. Bring to a simmer and cook, stirring occasionally for 30 minutes. Add broth as needed, if getting too thick.

Stir in the chicken and cook for 30 more minutes, or until the chicken is cooked and tender. Stir in the green onions, and add more broth to adjust to desired thickness. Cook for 2 minutes, and turn off heat. Taste for salt and spice, and adjust seasoning if needed. Serve with rice, if desired.

Healthy, delicious, fast, and cheap. What more could you want from a chicken dinner recipe?
Serve over rice, or, for a change of pace, toss with buttered noodles.

chicken broccoli stir-fry

serves 4

3 boneless, skinless chicken breasts

2 tablespoons cornstarch

2 tablespoons soy sauce

2 teaspoons minced ginger

3 cloves garlic, minced

3 tablespoons vegetable oil, divided

2 cups broccoli florets

1 cup thinly sliced carrots

1 small onion, cut into thin slices

1 cup chicken broth

Cut chicken into ½-inch thick strips, and transfer into a sealable plastic bag. Add cornstarch, soy sauce, ginger, and garlic to bag, and shake well. Refrigerate for 30 minutes.

In a large heavy skillet or wok, heat 2 tablespoons of oil over high heat. Stir-fry chicken until cooked through, about 4 minutes. Remove and reserve, covered with foil. Add remaining oil and stir-fry broccoli, celery, carrots, and onion for 5–6 minutes, or until almost tender. Add the broth and return chicken to pan. Cook, stirring for 2 minutes, until sauce thickens.

This classic chicken stew is easy to make, rustic, and delicious. Chicken cacciatore is great served over pasta, rice, or polenta.

hunter's chicken

serves 4

2 tablespoons olive oil

1 whole roasting chicken, cut into quarters

Salt and freshly ground black pepper, to taste

1 large onion, sliced

1 cup fresh mushrooms, quartered

4 garlic cloves, sliced

3 sprigs rosemary

1 teaspoon dried oregano

½ teaspoon red chile flakes, or to taste

1 cup tomato sauce

½ cup water

2 red bell peppers, sliced

2 green bell peppers, sliced

Preheat oven to 350°F.

Season the chicken generously with salt and freshly ground black pepper. Place a Dutch oven, over medium-high heat, add the olive oil and brown the chicken well on all sides.

Remove the chicken, add the onions, mushrooms, and garlic. Reduce the heat to medium, and sauté for about 5 minutes, until the onions turn translucent.

Stir in the rosemary, oregano, chile pepper flakes, tomato sauce, and water. Place the chicken and any juices, over the sauce, and top with the sliced peppers. Cover with the lid, and bake in the oven for 1 hour. Remove the lid for the final
15 minutes of cooking.

Remove and let rest, covered for 10 minutes. Skim any excess fat from the top of the sauce. Taste the sauce, and adjust seasoning with salt and pepper before serving. Serve over pasta, rice, or polenta.

This creamy and comforting chicken-noodle casserole is the epitome of classic home cooking.

chicken-noodle casserole

serves 6

3 tablespoons unsalted butter

½ yellow onion, finely diced

3 tablespoons all-purpose flour

3½ cups cold whole milk

One 10-ounce can condensed cream of mushroom soup

1 teaspoon salt

¼ teaspoon freshly ground black pepper

One 12-ounce package dry egg noodles

3 cups shredded cooked chicken, pulled from one roast chicken

¾ cup frozen peas, thawed, drained

1½ cups shredded Cheddar cheese

½ cup plain breadcrumbs

2 tablespoons olive oil

Preheat oven to 350°F.

Melt the butter in a medium saucepan, and sauté the onions over medium-low heat for about 4 minutes, or until translucent. Turn up the heat to medium; add the flour, and cook, stirring, for another 2 minutes. While whisking vigorously, slowly pour in 1 cup of the cold milk.

When the mixture begins to simmer, add the rest of the milk, soup, salt, and pepper. Cook, stirring occasionally, until the sauce thickens, and comes to a simmer. Remove from heat, and reserve.

Cook noodles in boiling salted water, 1 minute less than the directions call for. Drain well, and add to a large mixing bowl. Add the sauce, chicken, peas and about ⅔ of the cheese. Mix with a spatula to combine.

Pour the mixture into a lightly oiled 9x13 casserole dish, and top with the rest of the cheese. Mix the breadcrumbs and olive oil together in a small bowl until combined. Sprinkle evenly over the casserole. Bake for 35 minutes, or until browned and bubbly.

hunter's chicken

♣

page 158

chicken-noodle casserole

♣

page 159

This chicken pasta recipe is rich, decadent, delicious, and pretty quick to make. The big tip here is to splurge on real imported Italian cheese.

chicken carbonara

serves 6

1 tablespoon olive oil

6 strips bacon, chopped into small pieces

1 clove garlic, finely minced

2½ cups heavy cream

1¼ cup finely grated Parmesan

6 large egg yolks

¼ cup chopped fresh flat-leaf parsley

¼ cup chopped fresh basil

1 pound dried spaghetti

4 cups shredded cooked chicken (or amount from a large roasted chicken)

Salt and pepper, to taste

Heat olive oil in a large deep skillet over medium heat. Add bacon and cook until almost crisp. Turn off heat, and spoon off excess fat, leaving about 1 tablespoon in the pan.

In a mixing bowl, whisk together the garlic, cream, cheese, egg yolks, parsley and basil.

Bring a large pot of salted water to a rolling boil over high heat. Cook spaghetti 2 minutes less than according to package directions. Drain well.

Add the chicken to the skillet with the bacon, and stir to combine thoroughly. Add the hot spaghetti and cream/egg mixture, and toss constantly, cooking over medium-low heat until the chicken is heated through, the sauce thickens slightly, and the pasta finishes cooking, about 4–5 minutes. Do NOT boil. Reduce heat if needed during this step.

Season the pasta with pepper and salt, to taste. Serve immediately.

Chicken fettuccine Alfredo is easy to make at home. This recipe doesn't use butter and replaces some of the cream with chicken broth for a slightly lighter but just as delicious version. Do not make this unless you get real Parmigiano-Reggiano cheese!

chicken fettuccine alfredo

serves 4

2 cups low-sodium chicken broth

2 large chicken breasts

2 cups heavy cream

4 cloves garlic, very finely minced

2 large egg yolks

¼ cup chopped fresh flat-leaf parsley

2 cups freshly grated Parmigiano-Reggiano cheese, plus more for serving

Salt and freshly ground black pepper, to taste

1 pound fettuccine

Bring the chicken broth and breasts to a simmer in a small saucepan over medium heat. Cover, reduce the heat to low, and simmer for 12 minutes. Turn off the heat, and let sit in the hot broth for 15 minutes. When the chicken has cooled, cut into thin slices and reserve.

Put the pasta water on to boil.

Bring the chicken broth back to a boil over high heat. Cook until broth has reduced by half. Add the cream and garlic. When the mixture comes to a simmer, reduce the heat to low.

Beat the egg yolks in a small bowl. Slowly whisk in ½ cup of the hot cream mixture to warm the eggs. Turn off the heat, and whisk egg mixture into the cream sauce. Stir in the parsley and 1 cup of the cheese. Season with salt and freshly ground black pepper, to taste. Stir in sliced chicken. Cover, and reserve.

Boil the fettuccine in salted water, according to package directions. Drain well, but do not rinse. Quickly return pasta back into the pot, and pour over the sauce. Stir well, cover, and let sit 1 minute. Remove the cover, stir in last cup of cheese, and let sit for 1 more minute. Serve hot topped with additional grated cheese.

This recipe is based on the classic Chinese-American take-out dish Kung Pao chicken. We're using zucchini and peppers here, but almost any veggies will work in this recipe.

spicy peanut-chicken stir-fry

serves 4

2 tablespoons white wine, divided

2 tablespoons soy sauce, divided

2 tablespoon brown sugar, divided

1 pound boneless, skinless chicken breasts, cut into 1-inch cubes

½ cup chicken broth

2 teaspoons ketchup

1 tablespoon sesame oil

1 tablespoon Asian chili paste (sambal), or more to taste

1 tablespoon white vinegar

2 tablespoons rice vinegar

4 green onions, chopped, light and green parts separated

3 cloves garlic, minced

1 tablespoon vegetable oil

2 cups cubed zucchini

1 cup cubed red bell pepper

1 tablespoon cornstarch, dissolved in 2 tablespoons water

½ cup roasted, salted peanut halves

4 cups cooked white rice

Add 1 tablespoon of wine, 1 tablespoon of soy sauce, and 1 tablespoon of brown sugar to a mixing bowl. Add the chicken, and mix well. Cover, and refrigerate for 30 minutes.

In a small bowl, combine the chicken broth, ketchup, sesame oil, chili paste, vinegars, light parts of green onions, and garlic. Reserve.

Heat a large non-stick skillet over high heat. Add the vegetable oil, and when it starts to shimmer, add the chicken pieces. Stir-fry for about 4 minutes. Add the zucchini and red bell pepper. Stir-fry for another 3–4 minutes, or until vegetables begin to get tender. Add the sauce mixture, and cook for 3 minutes, or until the chicken and vegetables are cooked.

Stir in the cornstarch mixture, which will thicken the sauce quickly as it comes back to a simmer. When thick, turn off heat, and add peanuts and green onions. Taste, and adjust seasoning with more soy or chili sauce, as needed. Serve hot over rice.

Give visual interest and contrast to this delicious Hong Kong classic by making sure you use a red bell pepper rather than a green or yellow one.

chinese chicken on crispy noodles

serves 4

8 ounces boneless, skinless chicken breasts, shredded

1 large egg white

5 teaspoons cornstarch

8 ounces thin egg noodles

1²/₃ cups vegetable oil

2½ cups chicken stock

2 tablespoons dry sherry

2 tablespoons oyster sauce

1 tablespoon light soy sauce

1 tablespoon hoisin sauce

1 bell pepper, seeded and very thinly sliced

2 tablespoons water

3 green onions, chopped

Mix together the chicken, egg white, and 2 teaspoons of the cornstarch in a bowl. Let stand for at least 30 minutes.

Blanch the noodles in boiling water for 2 minutes, then drain thoroughly.

Heat the vegetable oil in a preheated wok. Add the noodles, spreading them to cover the base of the wok. Cook over low heat for about 5 minutes, until the noodles are browned on the underside. Flip the noodles over and brown on the other side. Remove from the wok when crisp and browned, place on a serving plate, and keep warm. Drain the oil from the wok.

Add 1¼ cups of the stock to the wok. Remove from the heat and add the chicken, stirring well so that it does not stick. Return to the heat and cook for 2 minutes. Drain, discarding the stock.

Wipe the wok with paper towels and return to the heat. Add the sherry, sauces, bell pepper, and remaining stock and bring to a boil. Blend the remaining cornstarch with the water and stir it into the mixture.

Return the chicken to the wok and cook over low heat for 2 minutes. Place the chicken on top.

There are many variations of this Creole classic, but this sausage-and-chicken version is a real crowd favorite. The nutritious brown rice adds a great texture and nutty flavor.

chicken jambalaya with brown rice

serves 4

2 tablespoons butter

4 ounces Andouille sausage, or other spicy smoked sausage, sliced ¼-inch thick

2 tablespoons paprika

1 tablespoon ground cumin

½ teaspoon cayenne pepper

½ teaspoon freshly ground black pepper

1 teaspoon salt

½ cup diced tomato, fresh or canned

1 large green bell pepper, diced

2 stalks celery, sliced ¼-inch thick

4 green onions, sliced thin

1 cup brown rice

3 cups chicken broth

1 pound chicken, boneless, skinless breasts or thighs, cut in ½-inch cubes

In a heavy-bottomed pot with a lid, melt the butter over medium heat. Add the sliced sausage and cook, stirring, for 5 minutes. Add the paprika, cumin, cayenne, black pepper, and salt. Sauté the spices for 1 minute, and then add the tomatoes. Cook, stirring for a few minutes to let some of the liquid evaporate. Add the green bell pepper, celery, and most of the green onions (reserve some of the dark green parts of the onions for the top). Cook, stirring for 5 minutes.

Stir in the rice, and mix well. Add the broth and chicken, turn the heat up to high, and bring to a simmer. Reduce the heat to low, cover the pot, and cook for 45 minutes. Remove the lid and check the rice. It should be just tender; if it is still too firm, cook longer. Serve with green onions sprinkled on top.

Note: If you decide to substitute white rice, you'll need to check the rice after 20 minutes, as it cooks much faster than brown rice.

Pasta, mushrooms, chicken, cream—there's a reason why some dishes become classics and stay that way.

chicken and mushroom tagliatelle

serves 4

10 ounces (1¼ cups) dried shiitake mushrooms

1½ cups hot water

1 tablespoon olive oil

6 bacon strips, chopped

3 boneless, skinless chicken breasts (roughly 6 ounces each), cut into strips

2 cups fresh shiitake mushrooms, sliced

1 small onion, finely chopped

1 teaspoon finely chopped fresh oregano or marjoram

1 cup chicken stock

1¼ cups heavy cream

1 pound dried tagliatelle

½ cup freshly grated Parmesan cheese

Salt and pepper, to taste

Chopped fresh flat-leaf parsley, to garnish

Put the dried mushrooms in a bowl with the hot water. Let soak for 30 minutes, or until softened. Remove, squeezing excess water back into the bowl. Strain the liquid through a fine-mesh strainer, and reserve. Slice the soaked mushrooms, discarding the stems.

Heat the oil in a large skillet over medium heat. Add the bacon and chicken, then cook for about 3 minutes. Add the dried and fresh mushrooms, onion, and oregano. Cook for 5–7 minutes, or until soft. Pour in the stock and the reserved mushroom liquid. Bring to a boil, stirring. Simmer for about 10 minutes, continuing to stir, until reduced. Add the cream, and simmer for 5 minutes, stirring, until beginning to thicken. Season with salt and pepper, to taste. Remove the skillet from the heat, and set aside.

Meanwhile, bring a large pot of lightly salted water to a boil. Add the pasta, bring back to a boil, and cook for 8–10 minutes, or according to the package directions, until tender but still firm to the bite. Drain, and transfer to a serving dish. Pour the sauce over the pasta. Add half the Parmesan cheese, and mix. Sprinkle with parsley and serve with the remaining Parmesan.

These meatballs are so delicious that you'll forget they're much healthier than ones made with beef and pork. Serve in your favorite pasta sauce.

chicken meatballs and pasta

serves 8

2 pounds ground chicken

¾ cup Parmesan cheese

½ cup plain breadcrumbs

2 large eggs

4 cloves garlic, finely minced

⅓ cup chopped fresh flat-leaf parsley

1 teaspoon dried oregano

½ teaspoon dried basil

1½ teaspoon salt, or to taste

Pinch of cayenne pepper

3 tablespoons olive oil, for frying

2 quarts prepared pasta sauce

Place all the ingredients, except the olive oil and pasta sauce, into a large mixing bowl. Mix together until evenly combined. Form mixture into 1-inch meatballs.

In large skillet, heat olive oil over medium-high heat. Brown the meatballs in batches on all sides. Transfer meatballs into a pot of pasta sauce as they are done. Simmer on low for 30 minutes, or until cooked through. Serve over pasta.

The perfect risotto requires risotto rice. The grains of this rice are short and absorb liquid without becoming too soft. Don't even thinking about using another rice.

chicken risotto

serves 4

9 tablespoons unsalted butter

2 pounds boneless, skinless chicken breasts, thinly sliced

1 large onion, chopped

2½ cups risotto rice

½ cup white wine

1 teaspoon crumbled saffron threads

5¼ cups hot chicken stock

½ cup Parmesan cheese, grated

Pinch of salt

Freshly ground black pepper, to taste

Heat 4 tablespoons butter in a deep saucepan. Add the chicken and onion, and cook, stirring frequently, for 8 minutes, or until golden-brown.

Add the rice, and mix to coat in the butter. Cook, stirring constantly, for 2–3 minutes, or until the grains are translucent.

Add the wine, and cook, stirring constantly, for 1 minute, until reduced.

Mix the saffron with ¼ cup of the hot stock. Add the liquid to the rice, and cook, stirring constantly, until it is absorbed.

Gradually add the remaining hot stock, a ladleful at a time. Add more liquid as the rice absorbs each addition. Cook stirring, for 20 minutes, or until all the liquid is absorbed and the rice is creamy.

Remove from the heat and add the remaining butter. Mix well, and then stir in the Parmesan until it melts. Season with salt and pepper, to taste.

Spoon the risotto into warmed serving dishes, and serve immediately.

This easy Bolognese recipe is so tasty you'll forget you used ground chicken instead of beef! This Bolognese is a light version of the classic Italian sauce.

chicken rigatoni bolognese

serves 6

3 tablespoons olive oil

2 pounds ground chicken

1 onion, chopped

4 cloves garlic, minced

2 teaspoons dried Italian herbs, to taste

1 teaspoon salt, or to taste

Freshly ground black pepper, to taste

$\frac{1}{3}$ cup whole milk

One 28-ounce jar marinara sauce

2 cups water, and more as needed

½ bunch fresh flat-leaf parsley, chopped

1 pound rigatoni

Grated Parmesan cheese, for serving

In a large saucepan, add the oil and sauté the chicken and onions over medium heat until the onions soften, about 10 minutes. As it cooks, break up the chicken into very small pieces (the smaller the better) with the back of a wooden spoon. Add the garlic, herbs, salt, pepper, and milk. Cook, stirring for 2 minutes.

Add the marinara sauce, water, and parsley. Simmer uncovered on medium-low for 1 hour, or until the chicken is very tender. Add more water, as needed, while it cooks to keep the sauce from getting too thick.

Boil the rigatoni according to directions, and then drain thoroughly. Stir the pasta into sauce, turn off the heat, and stir in the cheese; cover and let sit for 2 minutes before serving.

6

BEST ROAST CHICKEN

The perfect roast chicken has a crispy, buttery skin. This recipe delivers just that.

italian-style roast chicken

serves 6

1 whole chicken (6 pounds)

Sprigs of fresh rosemary

¾ cup coarsely grated feta cheese

2 tablespoons sun-dried tomato paste

4 tablespoons unsalted butter, softened

Salt and freshly ground black pepper,
to taste

1 head garlic

2 pounds 4 ounces new potatoes (halved,
if large)

1 each red, green, and yellow bell pepper,
seeded and cut into chunks

3 zucchini, thinly sliced

2 tablespoons olive oil

2 tablespoons all-purpose flour

2½ cups chicken stock

Preheat the oven to 375°F.

Rinse the chicken inside and out with cold water and drain well. Carefully cut between the skin and the top of the breast meat using a small pointed knife. Slide a finger into the slit and carefully enlarge it to form a pocket. Continue until the skin is completely lifted away from both breasts and the top of the legs.

Chop the leaves from 3 rosemary sprigs. Mix with the feta cheese, tomato paste, butter, and pepper to taste, and then spoon under the skin. Put the chicken in a large roasting pan, cover with foil, and cook for 20 minutes per 1 pound, plus 20 minutes.

Break the head of garlic into cloves, but do not peel. Add the vegetables and garlic to the chicken after 40 minutes, drizzle with oil, tuck in a few sprigs of rosemary, and season with salt and pepper. Cook for the remaining calculated time, removing the foil for the last 40 minutes to brown the chicken.

Transfer the chicken to a serving platter. Place some of the vegetables around the chicken, and transfer the remainder to a warmed serving dish.

Spoon the fat (it will be floating on top) out of the roasting pan, and discard. Stir the flour into the remaining cooking juices. Place the roasting pan on top of the stove, and cook over medium heat for 2 minutes, then gradually stir in the stock. Bring to a boil, stirring, until thickened. Strain into a gravy boat, and serve with the chicken.

Chipotle chile powder is made from dried jalepeño chile peppers that are smoked over a wood fire. It gives this roast chicken a spicy, slightly smoky flavor.

whole roasted chipotle chicken

serves 4

1 tablespoon vegetable oil

2 teaspoons chipotle chile powder

1 teaspoon ground cumin

½ teaspoon dried oregano

2 tablespoons fresh lime juice

Salt and freshly ground black pepper, to taste

1 whole chicken (4–5 pounds)

1 large white onion, sliced thin

½ cup chicken stock or broth

Preheat oven to 400°F.

In a large mixing bowl, combine the vegetable oil, chipotle chile powder, cumin, dried oregano, lime juice, salt, and pepper. Whisk together, and add the chicken to the bowl. Turn the chicken to coat on all sides. Rub the cavity with any excess spice mixture, and tie the legs together with a piece of kitchen string.

Add the onions to the bottom of a heavy-duty 9x13–inch metal or glass baking dish. Place the chicken on top of the onions. Roast for 1 hour and 15 minutes, or until an internal temperature of 165°F is reached.

Transfer the chicken to a plate to rest, and cover loosely with foil. Add the chicken stock to the baking dish, and scrape the bottom of the pan to deglaze any of the caramelized juices. Strain the liquid into a bowl. Taste for seasoning, and adjust if needed. Cut the chicken into serving pieces, and serve with the pan juices on the side.

The keys to this great recipe are roasting in a nice hot oven and using a roasting pan you can also make the sauce in after the chicken is cooked.

garlic-and-rosemary roast chicken with pan gravy

serves 4

6 cloves garlic

Salt and freshly ground black pepper, to taste

¼ cup olive oil

2 tablespoons minced fresh rosemary leaves

1 teaspoon dried Italian herbs

1 whole chicken (about 5 pounds) rinsed, dried with paper towels

1½ cups chicken stock

1 tablespoon unsalted butter

Crush garlic cloves with the flat of a knife, and remove the skin. Mince garlic very fine. Add a pinch of salt, and using the flat of the knife, scrape and press the garlic against the cutting surface to make a smooth paste.

Add the olive oil to a large mixing bowl with the garlic, rosemary, and dried Italian herbs. Mix thoroughly. Add the chicken to the bowl and rub it all over, including inside the cavity, with the garlic and herb oil. You can continue the recipe at this point, or leave the chicken to marinate in the fridge for a few hours, or even overnight.

Preheat oven to 400°F.

Place the chicken in a large, ovenproof skillet, or other heavy-duty metal roasting pan. Choose something that can also be placed over a flame on top of the stove later. Season the cavity generously with salt and freshly ground black pepper. Tie the legs together with kitchen string.

Season the outside generously with more salt and pepper. Place in the center of the oven and roast for 1 hour, or until a thermometer inserted in the thickest part of a thigh registers 165°F. Carefully transfer the chicken to a serving platter, and cover loosely with foil. Allow to rest for 10 minutes before serving.

While the chicken rests, make the pan sauce. Pour off the excess fat from the pan, and pour in the chicken stock. Place over high heat and bring to a boil, scraping all the caramelized pan drippings off the bottom with a whisk. Boil for 2 minutes, turn off the heat, and whisk in the cold butter. Season with salt and freshly ground black pepper, to taste. Serve alongside chicken.

This central New York specialty was invented by Dr. Robert Baker, a professor at New York's Cornell University, who wanted to create a delicious way to grill smaller chickens so that the local farms could sell more birds sooner.

cornell chicken

serves 4

For the basting sauce:

2 cups cider vinegar

1 cup vegetable oil

1 egg

3 tablespoons salt

½ teaspoon freshly ground black pepper

1 tablespoon poultry seasoning

2 whole chickens (2½–3 pounds each), cut in half

Combine the basting-sauce ingredients in a blender, and blend well. Place chicken halves in a large zip-top plastic bag and pour in 1/2 cup of the sauce. Reserve remaining sauce. Seal and shake bag gently to coat the chicken evenly. Refrigerate overnight.

Remove the chicken from the marinade, and wipe off excess sauce from the surface. Grill over charcoal, over indirect heat, turning and liberally basting with some of the reserved sauce every 10 minutes, for about 1 hour, or until cooked through.

Recipe makes enough basting sauce for about 4 whole chickens, and any extra can be stored in the refrigerator for several weeks.

Why dirty another dish? Here we're roasting the yams around the chicken for a delicious combination of sweet and savory.

whole roasted chicken and yams

serves 4

3 tablespoons olive oil

1 teaspoon dried thyme

1 teaspoon dried sage

1 teaspoon dried rosemary

Juice of 1 lemon

1 whole chicken (4–5 pounds)

Salt and freshly ground black pepper, as needed

1½ pounds yams or sweet potatoes, peeled, cut into 2- to 3-inch pieces

Preheat oven to 425°F.

In a large mixing bowl, combine the olive oil, dried herbs, and lemon juice. Whisk together, and add the chicken to the bowl. Turn the chicken to coat on all sides. Transfer chicken to a large roasting pan. Season with salt and pepper to taste, inside and out, and tie the legs together with a piece of kitchen string.

Add the yams to the mixing bowl, and toss to coat with the remaining oil and herbs. Scatter evenly around the chicken. Place in the preheated oven, and roast for 1 hour and 10 minutes, or until an internal temperature of 165°F is reached.

Transfer the chicken to a platter, cover loosely with foil, and let rest for 10 minutes. Cut the chicken into serving pieces, and serve with the roasted vegetables alongside.

This great roast-chicken recipe is rustic and simple but has big flavor. The herbs, lemon, and garlic combine to make a warm dressing for the chicken and watercress.

lemon, herb and garlic roast chicken with watercress

serves 4

2 lemons, halved, juiced and halves reserved

4 sprigs thyme

2 sprigs rosemary

6 cloves garlic, crushed, unpeeled

Salt and freshly ground black pepper, as needed

1 whole chicken (4–5 pounds)

1 onion, sliced

1 tablespoon olive oil

½ cup chicken stock or broth

2 tablespoons walnut or hazelnut oil

2 bunches watercress, stemmed, washed and dried

Preheat oven to 400°F.

In a large mixing bowl, add the lemons and juice, thyme, rosemary, garlic, salt, and black pepper. Whisk together, and add the chicken to the bowl. Turn the chicken to coat on all sides. Fill the cavity with the contents of the bowl, and tie the legs together with a piece of kitchen string.

Choose a heavy-duty 9x13–inch metal or flame-proof ceramic baking dish, and add the onions to the bottom. Place the chicken in the baking dish, and pour over the rest of the liquid. Drizzle the chicken with olive oil, and season generously with salt, and roast for 1 hour and 15 minutes, or until chicken reaches an internal temperature of 165°F.

Transfer the chicken to a plate, and cover with foil again while you make the sauce. Add the chicken stock to the baking dish, and scrape the bottom of the pan to deglaze any of the caramelized juices. Strain the liquid into a bowl, add the walnut or hazelnut oil, and whisk to combine. Pour any juices that have collected on the plate under the chicken. Taste for salt and freshly ground black pepper, and adjust seasoning.

To serve, toss the watercress in a large bowl with half of the hot sauce to wilt it very slightly. Divide the greens on plates. Cut the chicken into serving pieces, and top the watercress. Spoon over the remaining sauce.

Chinese five-spice powder is an amazing ingredient and gives this simple roast chicken a deep, exotic flavor. You'll also love how great it makes your kitchen smell as the chicken roasts!

whole roasted five-spice chicken

serves 4

1 tablespoon vegetable oil

1 tablespoon Chinese five-spice powder

1 teaspoon Asian-style hot sauce

Salt and freshly ground black pepper, as needed

1 whole chicken (4–5 pounds)

1 onion, sliced

½ cup chicken stock or broth

Preheat oven to 400°F.

In a large mixing bowl, combine the vegetable oil, Chinese five-spice powder, hot sauce, salt and pepper. Whisk together, and add the chicken to the bowl. Turn the chicken to coat on all sides. Fill the cavity with the excess, and tie the legs together with a piece of kitchen string.

In a heavy-duty 9x13–inch metal or ceramic baking dish, add the onions to the bottom. Roast in oven for 1 hour and 15 minutes, or until an internal temperature of 165°F.

Transfer the chicken to a plate, and cover loosely with foil. Add the chicken stock to the baking dish, and scrape the bottom of the pan to deglaze any of the caramelized juices. Strain the liquid into a bowl. Taste for seasoning, adjusting if needed.

Cut the chicken into serving pieces, and serve with the pan juices on the side.

lemon, herb and garlic roast chicken
with watercress

page 188

whole roasted five-spice chicken

page 189

Pork sausage and cornbread combine to make this roasted whole chicken something very special. Be sure to use the dried, savory type of cornbread for this, as the sweeter styles will not work as well.

sausage cornbread-stuffed chicken

serves 4

8 ounces pork sausage, casing removed, crumbled

1 tablespoon unsalted butter

1 onion, diced

1 stalk celery, diced

2 tablespoons chopped fresh flat-leaf parsley

½ teaspoon salt

½ teaspoon black pepper

2 cups crumbled cornbread

1 large egg, beaten

½ cup chicken broth

1 whole roasting chicken (about 4–5 pounds)

1 tablespoon melted unsalted butter

Salt and pepper, to taste

Preheat oven to 375°F.

In a skillet, sauté the sausage over medium heat until cooked through. Use a wooden spoon to break the meat into small pieces as it cooks. Drain the grease, and add butter, onion and celery, and sauté until translucent. Add parsley, salt and pepper, cornbread, egg and chicken broth, and mix thoroughly.

Spoon stuffing into cavity of chicken, and tie the legs together with kitchen string to hold the stuffing in. Rub chicken with melted butter, and season with salt and pepper, to taste.

Place chicken in a roasting pan. Roast for about 1 hour and 20 minutes, basting occasionally, until done, and an internal temperature of 170° F is reached. Let chicken rest for 15 minutes before serving.

Honey mustard is a very popular dip for things like wings and chicken fingers, but it also makes a great glaze for a slow-roasted whole chicken.

whole roasted honey-mustard chicken

serves 4

1 whole chicken (4–5 pounds)

Salt and pepper, to taste

1 tablespoon vegetable oil

2 tablespoons honey

¼ cup Dijon mustard

⅛ teaspoon cayenne pepper

Preheat oven to 325°F.

Season cavity of the chicken generously with salt and pepper. Tie the legs together with a piece of kitchen string. Place on a wire rack in a roasting pan. Pour a cup of water in the bottom of the pan to prevent the dripping honey mustard from burning.

Whisk together the rest of the ingredients. Use a brush to paint the glaze over the entire surface of the chicken. Season the skin with salt and pepper. Roast for 2 hours, or until an internal temperature of 165°F is reached. You can tent the chicken loosely with foil if the skin is getting too dark for your liking.

The salty, briny goodness of olives and capers is a perfect anecdote to the too-often bland taste of roast chicken. The pan juices are great over rice.

whole roast chicken
with olives and capers

serves 4

1 tablespoon vegetable oil

1 teaspoon ground cumin

½ teaspoon dried oregano

½ teaspoon dried thyme

2 tablespoons fresh lemon juice

⅛ teaspoon red-pepper flakes

Salt and freshly ground black pepper, to taste

1 whole chicken (4–5 pounds)

1 large white onion, sliced thin

½ cup halved Kalamata olives

¼ cup whole capers, drained

2 cups chicken broth

Water, as needed

Preheat oven to 400°F.

In a large mixing bowl, combine the vegetable oil, cumin, oregano, thyme, lemon juice, red-pepper flakes, salt, and pepper. Whisk together, and add the chicken to the bowl. Turn the chicken to coat on all sides. Rub the cavity with any excess spice mixture, and tie the legs together with a piece of kitchen string.

In a heavy-duty metal roasting pan or large ceramic baking dish, add the onions, olives, capers, and chicken broth. Place the chicken on top of the onions. Roast for 1 hour and 15 minutes, or until an internal temperature of 165°F is reached. During cooking, add enough water periodically to prevent the pan from drying out.

Transfer the chicken to a plate to rest, and cover loosely with foil. Pour the contents from the roasting pan into a saucepan. Skim excess fat from the top. Add enough water or broth to make about 2 cups of liquid total. Place over medium-high heat. Bring to a boil, and cook for about 5 minutes, or until reduced by about one-third.

Taste for seasoning, and adjust if needed. Cut the chicken into serving pieces, and spoon olives and capers over. Drizzle with the reduced pan juices, and serve immediately.

Any summer squash will work in this recipe, even the humble green zucchini. The orange zest adds a nice flavor and aroma to the final dish.

orange-scented roast chicken and summer squash

serves 4

3 tablespoons olive oil

2 teaspoons Dijon mustard

1 teaspoon dried tarragon

Juice of 1 orange

Finely grated zest of 1 orange

1 whole chicken (4–5 pounds)

Salt and freshly ground black pepper, as needed

1½ pounds summer squash, cut into 3-inch pieces

Preheat oven to 425°F.

In a large mixing bowl, combine the olive oil, mustard, tarragon, orange juice, and zest. Whisk together, and add the chicken to the bowl. Turn the chicken to coat on all sides. Transfer chicken to a large roasting pan. Season with salt and pepper, inside and out, and tie the legs together with a piece of kitchen string.

Add the summer squash to the mixing bowl, and toss to coat with the remaining oil mixture. Season with salt and pepper, to taste. Scatter evenly around the chicken. Place in the preheated oven, and roast for 1 hour 10 minutes, or until an internal temperature of 165°F is reached.

Remove chicken from oven and transfer to a platter, covering loosely with foil. Let rest for 10 minutes. Cut the chicken into serving pieces, and serve with the roasted squash alongside.

This easy chicken recipe is basically made with three ingredients found in almost any refrigerator, often inside the door (hence the name). This version uses an Asian-style salad dressing, but any style will work.

fridge-door chicken thighs

serves 4

2 tablespoons ketchup

1 tablespoon yellow mustard

4 cloves garlic, finely minced

½ teaspoon red-pepper flakes

⅔ cup Asian sesame salad dressing (or other salad dressing)

8 chicken thighs, bone-in, skin on

Salt and freshly ground black pepper, to taste

Add the first 5 ingredients to a large bowl, and mix to combine. To prepare the chicken thighs, trim away excess fat, turn them skin-side up, and make 2 deep slashes on each, all the way to the bone.

Add chicken to the marinade, toss to coat completely, cover, and refrigerate at least 8 hours, or overnight.

Preheat oven to 400°F.

Remove chicken from marinade, wiping off any excess liquid. Season with salt and freshly ground black pepper, to taste. Place on a foil-lined pan, and roast chicken for about 45 minutes or until it reaches an internal temperature of 170°F. Allow to rest for 10 minutes before serving.

This once popular dish is back in style—the perfect midweek winter warmer. Serve with mashed potatoes or boiled rice to soak up the delicious juices.

winter pot roast chicken

serves 4

2 tablespoons sunflower oil

2 tablespoons unsalted butter

1 whole chicken (3 pounds)

Salt and pepper

1½ cups diced parsnips

1½ cups diced rutabaga

1½ cups diced carrots

6 shallots, halved

2 cups chicken stock

3 tablespoons pearl barley

1 bouquet garni

Fresh thyme sprigs, to garnish

Preheat the oven to 325°F. Heat 1 tablespoon of the oil and the butter in a large deep skillet. Season the chicken well with salt and pepper and cook in the hot fat, turning, for 7–8 minutes, until lightly browned. Transfer to a large casserole.

Add the remaining oil to the skillet and stir in the diced vegetables and shallots. Cook over medium–high heat, stirring, for 10 minutes. Add the stock and pearl barley, then bring to a boil. Reduce the heat, simmer for 5 minutes, then transfer to the casserole. Add the bouquet garni and season to taste with salt and pepper.

Cover and cook in the preheated oven for 1¼ hours. Uncover the casserole and cook for an additional 20 minutes, until all the vegetables are tender, the chicken is golden, and the juices run clear when a sharp knife is inserted into the thickest part of the meat. Garnish with thyme sprigs and serve immediately.

The only thing better than a fragrant, beautifully browned roast chicken is one served with a rich, freshly made pan gravy. The keys to this great recipe are a very hot oven and a roasting pan that you can also make the sauce in after the chicken is cooked.

whole roast garlic-herb chicken with pan gravy

serves 4

4 garlic cloves

1/3 cup olive oil

2 teaspoons very finely minced fresh thyme leaves

2 teaspoons very finely minced fresh rosemary leaves

1 teaspoon dried Italian herbs

1 large whole chicken (about 5 pounds), rinsed and dried with paper towels

Salt and freshly ground black pepper, to taste

For the gravy:

1½ tablespoons reserved chicken fat

1 tablespoon unsalted butter

1 heaping tablespoon all-purpose flour

2 cups cold chicken broth

½ teaspoon balsamic vinegar

4 sprigs fresh thyme

Salt and freshly ground black pepper, to taste

Preheat oven to 450°F.

Remove skins and crush the garlic cloves with the flat of a knife. Mince and press until it is a very fine paste.

Add garlic, olive oil, thyme, rosemary and dried Italian herbs to a large mixing bowl. Rub the chicken inside and out with the mixture. Continue or leave to marinade overnight or for a few hours.

Place chicken in an ovenproof skillet or roasting pan (something that can be used on the stove top later) and roast for 1 hour, or until a thermometer registers 165°F. Remove the chicken, place on a platter, and cover with foil. Allow to rest while making the gravy.

Pour the excess chicken fat from the pan, leaving 1½ tablespoons behind. Place back on the stove, and add the butter. When the butter melts, add a little flour, and cook, stirring with a whisk constantly until golden-brown. Whisk in 2 cups of cold chicken broth, the balsamic vinegar, and thyme. Turn the heat to high, and boil for 5 minutes, stirring until the gravy is thickened. Season with salt and pepper, to taste.

The picture of home cooking is a whole roast chicken stuffed with a classic bread-and-herb stuffing hot from the oven, sitting in the middle of a large table.

whole roast chicken stuffed with herb stuffing

serves 4

4 tablespoons unsalted butter

1 onion, diced

1 stalk celery, diced

½ teaspoon dried leaf thyme

2 tablespoon chopped fresh flat-leaf parsley

½ teaspoon salt

½ teaspoon black pepper

2 cups fresh crumbled breadcrumbs

1 large egg, beaten

2 tablespoons whole milk

¼ cup chicken broth

1 large whole roasting chicken (about 4–5 pounds)

1 tablespoon melted unsalted butter

Salt and pepper, to taste

Preheat oven to 375°F.

In a skillet, melt butter over medium heat, and sauté onion and celery until translucent. Add thyme, parsley, salt and pepper, and breadcrumbs. Stir to combine, and then mix in egg, milk, and chicken broth to make a moist stuffing.

Spoon stuffing into cavity of chicken, and tie the legs together with kitchen string to hold the stuffing in. Rub chicken with melted butter, and season with salt and pepper to taste.

Place chicken in a roasting pan. Roast for about 1 hour and 20 minutes, basting occasionally, until done, and chicken reaches an internal temperature of 170°F. Let chicken rest for 15 minutes before serving.

Smoky bacon and earthy sage combine to flavor this roasted whole chicken from the inside out. If bacon's not your thing, no worries, just leave it out—this is still a great all-purpose stuffed-chicken recipe.

bacon-sage stuffed chicken

serves 4

6 strips bacon, sliced in ¼-inch pieces

1 onion, diced

1 stalk celery, diced

¼ cup fresh sage leaves, chopped

2 tablespoon chopped fresh flat-leaf parsley

½ teaspoon salt

½ teaspoon black pepper

2 cups dried plain bread cubes or croutons

1 large egg, beaten

½ cup chicken broth

1 large whole roasting chicken (about 4–5 pounds)

1 tablespoon melted unsalted butter

Salt and pepper, to taste

In a skillet, cook bacon over medium heat until almost crisp. Add onion and celery and sauté until translucent. Add sage, parsley, salt and pepper, bread cubes, egg, and chicken broth, and mix thoroughly.

Spoon stuffing into cavity of chicken, and tie the legs together with kitchen string to hold the stuffing in. Rub chicken with melted butter, and season with salt and pepper to taste. Place chicken in a roasting pan. Roast at 375°F for about 1 hour and 20 minutes, basting occasionally, until done, and an internal temperature of 170°F is reached. Let chicken rest for 15 minutes before serving.

Nothing complicated about this simple one-dish meal. The hot oven really locks in the flavors, and the little touch of sherry vinegar at the end brings everything together.

roasted chicken and red potatoes

serves 4

¼ cup olive oil

2 cloves garlic, finely minced

2 tablespoons chopped flat-leaf parsley

1 teaspoon dried rosemary

1 teaspoon dried thyme

1 teaspoon Dijon mustard

Pinch of cayenne pepper

1 onion, sliced thin

1 whole chicken, cut into 8 serving-sized pieces

2½ pounds small red potatoes, washed

Salt and freshly ground black pepper, to taste

2 tablespoons sherry vinegar

Preheat oven to 425°F.

Add the olive oil, garlic, parsley, rosemary, dried thyme, Dijon mustard, and cayenne to a mixing bowl. Whisk to combine.

Place the onion, chicken, and potatoes in a large roasting pan. Pour over the herb mixture, and use your hands to toss everything together. Space out chicken pieces as evenly from each other as possible.

Season entire pan generously with salt and pepper. Roast for 45 minutes, or until the potatoes are tender and the chicken has reached an internal temperature of 165°F. Remove, and transfer chicken to a serving platter.

Add the sherry vinegar to the roasting pan, and use a spatula to toss everything together. Add potato mixture to the platter of chicken, and serve.

bacon-sage stuffed chicken

page 206

roasted chicken and red potatoes

page 207

The Greeks have been roasting chicken with herbs and garlic like this since ancient times. It's so delicious, there's no reason to stop now.

greek herb roast chicken

serves 4

¼ cup olive oil

3 cloves garlic, chopped

1 tablespoon chopped fresh rosemary

1 tablespoon chopped fresh thyme

1 tablespoon chopped fresh oregano

1 tablespoon chopped fresh marjoram

Juice of 2 lemons

1 whole chicken (4 pounds), cut into pieces

Salt and freshly ground black pepper, to taste

In a large glass baking dish, mix the olive oil, garlic, rosemary, thyme, oregano, marjoram, and lemon juice. Add the chicken pieces and toss in the mixture. Sprinkle generously with salt and pepper. Wrap tightly in plastic, and marinate overnight in the refrigerator.

Preheat oven to 425°F.

Place baking dish in preheated oven, and roast for 45 minutes, or until chicken reaches an internal temperature of 165°F. Remove, and let rest 5 minutes. Serve immediately, with any pan juices spooned over the top.

No subtle flavors here—just in-your-face spicy goodness. The fat from the Spanish chorizo sausage does most of the work in this easy roast-chicken recipe.

roasted spanish-style chicken with potatoes and sausage

serves 4–6

3 tablespoons olive oil

1 large roasting chicken, cut into 8 serving-sized pieces

1 large yellow onion, roughly chopped

1½ pounds small new potatoes, or larger ones cut into 2-inch chunks

1 pound chorizo sausage, cut into 1-inch pieces

1 teaspoon dried oregano

Freshly grated orange zest

Salt and pepper, to taste

Preheat the oven to 375°F.

Pour the oil in the bottom of a large roasting pan. Add the chicken, onions, potatoes, sausage, oregano, orange zest, and rub everything with the oil. Season with salt and pepper, to taste.

Roast for 30 minutes, remove, and use a spatula to toss the chicken and potatoes in the orange-colored fat that is released from the chorizo. Return to oven, and cook about 35 minutes more, or until the potatoes are tender and chicken is cooked through. Let rest 10 minutes before serving.

Sambal is an Asian-style hot sauce made from coarsely ground chiles, and is now commonly found in most large grocery stores. It's worth finding, if only to use in this recipe.

sambal-citrus roast chicken

serves 4

2 tablespoons vegetable oil

Juice of 1 orange

Juice of 1 lime

Juice of 1 lemon

1 tablespoon sambal chili paste

Salt and freshly ground black pepper, as needed

1 whole chicken (4–5 pounds), cut into 8 serving-sized pieces

¼ chopped cilantro

Preheat oven to 425°F.

In a large mixing bowl, combine all the ingredients, except the cilantro. Add the chicken pieces to the bowl, and toss to coat thoroughly.

Transfer chicken to a large roasting pan. Drizzle over any remaining sambal-citrus mixture, using a spatula to scrape the bowl clean.

Place in the preheated oven, and roast for 45 minutes, or until an internal temperature of 165°F is reached. Remove, and let rest 5 minutes. Scatter the chopped cilantro over the chicken. Serve immediately.

7

BRAISED, STEWED,
AND BAKED CHICKEN

This pepper-and-chicken stew recipe is as simple as it is comforting. You can make it as mild or spicy as you like by using any combination of peppers.

pepper-and-chicken stew

serves 4

1 whole chicken (about 4 pounds)

1 onion, chopped

2 red bell peppers, sliced into ½-inch strips

1 green bell pepper, sliced into ½-inch strips

2 jalapeño pepper, seeded and sliced

2 Roma tomatoes, sliced

2 cloves garlic, crushed

1 teaspoon oregano

1 bay leaf

Cayenne pepper, to taste

2 cups chicken broth

1 cup water

1 cup cream

1 teaspoon salt

½ teaspoon freshly ground black pepper

Fresh chopped flat-leaf parsley, to garnish (optional)

Combine all the ingredients (except parsley) in a pot large enough to fit the chicken. Bring to a simmer, turn the heat down to very low, cover, and simmer gently for 1½ hours.

Carefully remove chicken, and break into serving-size pieces. Skim the excess fat from the top of the broth, and add the chicken back in. Taste and adjust seasoning with extra cayenne, salt and pepper.

Serve in bowls, topped with chopped parsley.

This deliciously different dish shows the Moorish influence on many Spanish dishes—salty preserved lemons are a popular ingredient in North African cuisine.

spanish lemon chicken

serves 4

1 tablespoon all-purpose flour

Four 6-ounce chicken portions

2 tablespoons olive oil

2 garlic cloves, crushed

1 large Spanish onion, thinly sliced

3 cups chicken stock

½ teaspoon saffron threads

2 yellow bell peppers, seeded and cut into chunks

2 preserved lemons, cut into quarters

10 ounces brown basmati rice

Pinch white pepper

12 pimiento-stuffed green olives

Preheat the oven to 350°F.

Put the flour into a large freezer bag. Add the chicken, close the top of the bag, and shake to coat with flour.

Heat the oil in a large skillet over low heat, add the garlic, and cook for 1 minute, stirring constantly.

Add the chicken to the skillet and cook over medium heat, turning frequently, for 5 minutes, or until the skin is lightly browned, then remove to a plate. Add the onion to the skillet and cook, stirring occasionally, for 10 minutes until softened.

Meanwhile, put the stock and saffron into a pan over low heat and heat through. Transfer the chicken and onion to a large casserole dish, add the bell peppers, lemons, and rice, then pour over the stock. Mix well and season with pepper to taste.

Cover and cook in the preheated oven for 50 minutes, or until the chicken is cooked through and tender. Reduce the oven temperature to 325°F. Add the olives to the casserole and cook for an additional 10 minutes.

Your dreams have been answered: America's favorite Italian-American chicken dish is now available in casserole form.

chicken-parmesan casserole

serves 6

6 boneless, skinless chicken breasts (about 6–7 ounces each)

2 tablespoons olive oil

2 garlic cloves, finely minced

Red chile flakes, to taste

4 cups marinara sauce

¼ cup chopped basil

8 ounces shredded mozzarella, divided

4 ounces grated Parmesan

One 5-ounce package garlic croutons

Preheat the oven to 350°F.

Place the chicken breasts on a plate, and season both sides with salt and freshly ground black pepper. Set aside.

Spread the olive oil, garlic, and red chile flakes evenly on the bottom of a 9x13–inch casserole dish. Add 1 cup of the marinara sauce, and spread evenly. Place the chicken breasts in the dish, and space evenly so they cook uniformly. Top with the rest of the marinara sauce and basil.

Top with half the mozzarella and half the Parmesan. Pour over the croutons and spread evenly, top with the remaining cheese. Bake for 40 minutes or until top is browned and the chicken is cooked through.

Let rest for 5 minutes before serving with some sauce spooned from the bottom of the casserole.

Love fried chicken, but hate the mess on the stovetop? Try this oven method for a neater but still very tasty version.

oven-fried chicken

serves 6

1 cup all-purpose flour

1 teaspoon paprika

1 teaspoon salt

½ teaspoon black pepper

¼ teaspoon cayenne pepper

1 cup Italian-seasoned breadcrumbs

3 large eggs

12 chicken legs, bone in, skin on

⅓ cup vegetable oil

Preheat oven to 375°F.

Place flour in a shallow baking dish and stir in paprika, salt, pepper, and cayenne. Put the breadcrumbs in another shallow baking dish. Beat eggs in a separate mixing bowl.

Dredge the chicken in the flour piece by piece, dip in the egg, and then coat in the breadcrumbs, repeating until all pieces are done. Pour oil into a 9x13 baking dish. Add the chicken to the dish, and sprinkle with salt and pepper, to taste. Bake in the preheated oven for 25 minutes, remove, flip pieces over, and bake for another 25 minutes.

Remove from oven, and drain on a paper towel–lined baking rack. Serve immediately.

This North African–inspired chicken stew is rustic, easy to make, and exotically delicious. Try it served over couscous for an extra authentic touch.

moroccan chicken stew

serves 4

1 whole roasting chicken, cut into quarters

Salt and freshly ground black pepper, to taste

2 tablespoons olive oil

1 large onion, sliced

4 cloves garlic, sliced

1 teaspoon dried oregano

1 teaspoon cumin

1 teaspoon coriander

½ teaspoon cinnamon

½ teaspoon red chile flakes, or to taste

1 cup diced tomatoes

½ cup chicken broth

1 green bell pepper, sliced

2 tablespoons dried currants

2 tablespoons sliced almonds

Preheat oven to 350°F.

Season the chicken generously with salt and freshly ground black pepper. Place Dutch oven, over medium-high heat, add olive oil, and brown the chicken well on all sides. Remove the chicken, and add onions and garlic. Reduce the heat to medium, and sauté for about 5 minutes, until the onions turn translucent.

Stir in the rest of the ingredients. Place the chicken and any juices over the mixture. Cover with the lid, and bake for 1 hour and 15 minutes. Remove, and let rest for 15 minutes. Taste sauce, and adjust seasoning with salt and pepper before serving.

This is one of America's ultimate comfort foods. Some folks like their dumplings light and airy, while others prefer them more hearty and dense. These are somewhere in between, but every bit as delicious.

chicken and dumplings

serves 6

2 tablespoons vegetable oil

1 whole chicken (4–5 pounds is ideal), cut into quarters, backbone reserved

1 quart chicken broth

3 cups water

4 cloves garlic, peeled

1 bay leaf

4 sprigs fresh thyme

5 tablespoons unsalted butter

2 carrots, cut into ½-inch pieces

2 celery stalks, cut into ½-inch pieces

1 large onion, chopped

5 tablespoons all-purpose flour

1½ teaspoons salt

Freshly ground black pepper, to taste

Dash of hot sauce

For the dumplings:

1¾ cups all-purpose flour

1 teaspoon salt

2 teaspoons baking powder

¼ teaspoon baking soda

3 tablespoons cold unsalted butter

2 tablespoons thinly sliced green onion tops

¼ cup buttermilk

¾ cup whole milk

Place a heavy-bottomed Dutch oven over high heat, and add the vegetable oil. Brown the chicken pieces very well on all sides. When browned, add the broth, water, garlic, bay leaf, and thyme. As soon as it comes to a boil, turn the heat down to low and simmer, covered, for 30 minutes. Before covering, skim any foam that comes to the surface.

After 30 minutes, uncover, and carefully remove the chicken to a bowl to cool. Strain the liquid into another bowl and reserve. As it sits, you may skim off any fat that comes to the top.

Place the Dutch oven back on medium heat, and add the butter, carrots, celery, and onion. Sauté the vegetables in the butter for 5 minutes. Add the flour, and cook, stirring for about 2 minutes. Whisk in the reserved broth, one cup at a time. Add the salt, pepper, and hot sauce. Bring to a simmer, stirring occasionally. Reduce the heat to low, and simmer covered, for about 30 minutes, or until the vegetables are tender.

In the meantime, remove all the cooled chicken meat from the bones, and tear into large chunks. When the vegetables are done, stir in the chicken. Taste and adjust seasoning if needed. Cover, and reduce the heat to the lowest setting possible.

To make the dumplings: Add the flour, salt, baking powder, and baking soda to a mixing bowl. Stir with a whisk to combine. Add the cold butter, and cut in using a pastry blender until the mixture looks like coarse crumbs. Add the green onions, buttermilk, and milk, stirring with a fork just enough to form a thick, sticky dough.

Turn the heat under the Dutch oven up to medium. As soon as the mixture is simmering, give it a good stir, and drop the dumpling dough by large, rounded tablespoons onto the simmering chicken mixture, cover, and cook for 15 minutes. (No peeking!) The dumplings are done when they are firm and cooked in the middle. Turn off the heat, uncover, and serve hot.

You can make this in a casserole dish and serve it family-style, but there's something special about individual pot pies. With these, you always have a perfect balance between the filling and the buttery crust.

personal chicken pot pies

serves 6

8 ounces white button mushrooms, sliced

1 diced onion

1 tablespoon olive oil

2 cups sliced carrots

1 cup sliced celery

4 cups cold chicken broth, divided

6 tablespoons unsalted butter

½ cup all-purpose flour

2 pounds boneless, skinless chicken breasts, cut into 1-inch cubes

1 cup frozen green peas

1 teaspoon chopped fresh thyme leaves or a pinch of dried

1 teaspoon salt

¼ teaspoon black pepper

6 large (15-ounce) ramekins

Enough ready-made pie dough for two 10-inch pies (about 24 ounces)

1 egg, beaten

In a saucepan, sauté the mushrooms and onions in the olive oil over medium heat until golden. Add the carrots, celery, and 2 cups of chicken broth. Bring to a boil, reduce to low, and simmer until vegetables are almost tender.

Melt butter in another saucepan over medium heat. Whisk in the flour, and cook, stirring, for 3 minutes, or until the flour is a light tan color and smells like cooked piecrust. Slowly whisk in 2 cups of cold chicken broth. Simmer over medium heat until the mixture thickens. Remove and reserve.

Add vegetables and broth from the other pan when ready, and stir to combine. Add the chicken, peas, thyme, salt, and pepper. Bring back to a simmer and cook, stirring, for 5 minutes. Taste for seasoning, and set aside until needed.

Preheat oven to 400°F.

Divide the filling between the 6 ramekins (you should fill up to ½-inch from the top. Cut out circles of pie dough 1 inch larger than the width of the ramekins. Place the dough over the pot pies. Go around each piece of dough, folding a ½-inch over to form a rim. If desired, pinch with your fingertips to form a crimped edge. Cut a small "X" in the center of each crust.

Place the ramekins on a sheet pan. Brush the tops with the beaten egg. Bake for 40 minutes, or until pies are golden-brown and bubbly. Let sit for 10 minutes before serving.

chicken and dumplings

page 226

personal chicken pot pies

page 227

Breaded and fried chicken served with a lemon wedge is quite a nice treat, but when you add a center of melted garlic butter, it goes up to a whole other level of deliciousness.

chicken kiev

serves 6

6 tablespoons unsalted butter, room temperature

¼ cup chopped fresh flat-leaf parsley

3 cloves garlic, minced

¼ teaspoon salt

1 teaspoon freshly ground black pepper, divided

6 boneless, skinless chicken breasts

2 large eggs

2 tablespoons whole milk

1 cup all-purpose flour

Salt and pepper, to taste

¼ teaspoon ground black pepper

1 cup breadcrumbs

3 cups peanut oil, for frying

1 lemon, cut into 6 wedges

Combine butter, parsley, garlic, salt, and ½ teaspoon pepper in a mixing bowl. Spread on a piece of plastic wrap, and shape into a rectangle, about 3x6 inches wide. Wrap and place this mixture in freezer until firm.

Place each chicken breast between pieces of plastic wrap and pound to about ¼-inch thick. When butter is firm, remove from freezer and cut into 6 equal-sized pieces. Place a piece of butter on each breast. Fold edges of chicken in and roll to cover the butter completely. Secure the chicken roll with a few toothpicks.

In a mixing bowl, beat eggs and milk. In a separate bowl, mix together flour with salt and pepper to taste. Coat chicken with seasoned flour. Dip the floured chicken in egg mixture. Roll in breadcrumbs until coated thoroughly. Place chicken on a plate, and refrigerate uncovered for 1 hour.

Preheat peanut oil in a deep frying pan, over medium-high heat. Fry chicken for about 6–7 minutes per side, or until the chicken is golden-brown and cooked through. Serve immediately with lemon.

This classic stuffed-chicken recipe is named for the famous cooking school in France. Your guests will think you are a graduate when they taste this.

chicken cordon bleu

serves 4

1 cup all-purpose flour, seasoned generously with salt and freshly ground black pepper

3 large eggs, beaten

2 cups plain breadcrumbs

4 thin slices smoked ham

4 thin slices Swiss cheese

4 large boneless skinless chicken breasts, pounded to ¼-inch thick

Vegetable oil, for frying

Lemon wedges, for serving

Place the flour, eggs, and breadcrumbs in separate dishes for breading the chicken. Place a slice of ham and then cheese on each breast (should not be larger than pounded out breasts). Roll the chicken breasts up tightly, and fasten with 2–3 toothpicks to secure.

Preheat oven to 375°F.

Dip the chicken in the seasoned flour, then the beaten egg and lastly the breadcrumbs. Let rest on plate for 10 minutes, and heat the oil. In a skillet, heat ¼ inch of vegetable oil over medium-high heat. Place the chicken in the hot oil (seam side down) and fry for 2–3 minutes per side, until golden brown.

Transfer to a baking dish and place in the oven for 20 minutes, or until chicken is cooked through and reaches an internal temperature of 165°F. Serve with lemon wedges.

This Italian-style braised chicken recipe uses canned artichoke hearts for an easy but hearty meal. You'll want to have plenty of bread ready.

chicken braised with artichoke hearts

serves 4

1 large whole chicken, cut into serving size pieces

2 tablespoon olive oil

1 yellow onion, diced

4 cloves garlic, minced

1 teaspoon salt

One 14-ounce can butter beans, drained

1 red bell pepper, cut in 2-inch pieces

Juice from 1 lemon

1 teaspoon dried thyme

½ teaspoon dried oregano

1 teaspoon black pepper

¼ teaspoon red chile flakes

1 cup water

3 cups chicken stock or broth

Two 14-ounce cans artichoke hearts, drained

Season chicken pieces generously with salt and pepper. In a large Dutch oven, heat the olive oil on medium-high. When the oil is hot, brown the chicken well (in batches, if necessary). Reserve browned chicken, and add the onions, garlic, and salt. Reduce the heat to medium, and cook for 2–3 minutes.

Add the chicken back in, top with the rest of the ingredients, and artichoke hearts. Bring to a simmer, cover tightly and cook for 1 hour, stirring occasionally, until the chicken is fork-tender. Turn off heat, and taste for salt and pepper. Serve the chicken and artichoke hearts in bowls, topped with the broth.

This tasty cafeteria classic is great with the traditional beef, but also surprisingly good with chicken. Of course, the Italian pork sausage doesn't hurt.

chicken stuffed bell peppers

serves 4

For the sauce:

1 tablespoon olive oil

1 onion, diced

1 cup chicken broth

2½ cups prepared marinara sauce, or other tomato sauce

¼ teaspoon red chile flakes, optional

For the stuffed peppers:

1 pound lean ground chicken

½ pound sweet Italian pork sausage, casings removed

2 cups cooked rice

1 cup finely grated Parmesan (Parmigiano-Reggiano) cheese

¼ cup chopped fresh flat-leaf parsley

4 cloves garlic, very finely minced

One 10-ounce can diced tomatoes

2 teaspoons salt

1 teaspoon freshly ground black pepper

Pinch of cayenne pepper

4 large red bell peppers

To make the sauce, add the olive oil to a saucepan, and lightly brown the onions with a large pinch of salt over medium-high heat. Remove half and reserve for the stuffing. Stir in the rest of the sauce ingredients and bring to a simmer. Pour the sauce into the bottom of a large deep casserole dish.

Add all the filling ingredients to a mixing bowl, from the ground chicken to the cayenne, along with the reserved onions. Stir with a fork (or your hands) until the mixture is combined. Tip: Cook a small piece of the filling to test the seasoning.

Preheat oven to 375°F.

Cut the bell peppers in half lengthwise. Use a spoon to remove the stem, seeds and white membrane from each pepper. Place the bell peppers in the casserole dish, and fill each pepper with the stuffing. A little additional cheese can be grated over the top, if desired.

Cover with foil, and bake for 45 minutes. Remove foil and bake uncovered for another 20–30 minutes, or until the peppers are very tender. (Exact cooking time will depend on size, shape and thickness of the peppers.) Let rest for 10 minutes before serving. Serve with the sauce spooned over the top.

This easy chicken recipe is basically made with things you probably already have in the refrigerator. While it may seem unusual, it looks and tastes fantastic.

thousand-island chicken thighs

serves 4

½ cup Thousand Island salad dressing

2 teaspoons Dijon mustard

2 cloves garlic, finely minced

¼ teaspoon black pepper

1/8 teaspoon cayenne pepper

8 chicken thighs, bone-in, skin on

Salt and freshly ground black pepper, to taste

Add the first 5 ingredients to a large bowl, and mix to combine. To prep the chicken thighs, trim away excess fat, then turn them skin-side up and make 2 deep slashes on each, all the way to the bone.

Add the chicken to the marinade, toss to coat completely, cover, and refrigerate at least 4 hours, or overnight.

Preheat oven to 400°F.

Transfer chicken to a foil-lined pan. Season with salt and freshly ground black pepper to taste, and roast chicken for about 45 minutes or until it reaches an until an internal temperature of 170°F. Allow to rest for 5 minutes before serving.

This caramelized-onion chicken recipe is so easy to prepare, and the onion-and-garlic mixture keeps the chicken very moist and tender.

caramelized-onion and garlic chicken

serves 4

2 tablespoons olive oil

2 large onions, sliced

4 cloves garlic, minced

2 tablespoons brown sugar

2 tablespoons white-wine vinegar

Salt and pepper, to taste

4 split chicken breasts, bone-in

Heat olive oil in a large skillet over medium-low heat. Add the onion and garlic. Cook, stirring, for 10 minutes or until soft. Stir in sugar and vinegar and cook for about 5 minutes. Remove from heat. Season with salt and pepper, to taste.

Preheat oven to 425°F. Place chicken, bone side down, in a baking dish, season with salt and pepper, and spread onion mixture over the top of the chicken. Bake 20 to 25 minutes, or until it reaches an internal temperature of 165°F. Cover loosely with foil if the onions are getting too dark toward the end of the cooking time. Let rest for 5 minutes before serving.

Not the "sweet and sour" chicken you may be used to, but delicious nonetheless! You can also use peach preserves for this recipe, if you prefer.

chicken thighs with sweet-and-sour apricot sauce

serves 8

8 chicken thighs, skin on, bone in

Salt and freshly ground black pepper, to taste

1 tablespoon olive oil

1 yellow onion, sliced

1 carrot, sliced

1 stalk celery, sliced

6 whole garlic cloves, peeled and bruised

6 sprigs fresh thyme

1 cup chicken broth

For the apricot sauce:

1 cup apricot preserves

2 tablespoons rice vinegar

1 tablespoon water

1 teaspoon fresh thyme leaves

Coarsely ground black pepper, to taste

Salt, to taste

Preheat oven to 325°F.

Season the chicken thighs on both sides generously with salt and freshly ground black pepper. Heat the olive oil in a large ovenproof skillet on medium heat and place chicken in, skin-side down. Cook until skin is well browned, about 5 minutes. Turn over and brown the meat side for 3 minutes.

Transfer to a plate, pour off the excess fat, and add the vegetables, garlic, and thyme to the pan. Arrange the legs over the vegetables, skin-side up. Pour in the broth, cover with foil, and place the skillet in the oven.

Roast for 1 hour, or until the meat is almost fork-tender. Uncover, and turn the oven up to 425°F. Roast another 10 minutes. Remove from oven and let rest for 10 minutes before serving, topped with the apricot sauce.

For the apricot sauce: Add the preserves, rice vinegar, and water to a small saucepan. Bring to a simmer, stirring, over medium heat. Remove from heat and stir in the thyme, black pepper, and salt to taste. Serve warm or room temperature.

Let's face it— breaded chicken can be pretty dull, but that's not a problem here. The rich pistachios pair perfectly with the apricot sauce.

pistachio-crusted chicken with apricot

serves 4

For the sauce:

6 apricots, peeled, pitted, chopped

½ cup white wine

Salt and freshly ground black pepper, to taste

For the chicken:

¾ cup shelled pistachios, not salted

1 cup panko (Japanese breadcrumbs)

1 teaspoon paprika

1 teaspoon salt

4 boneless, skinless chicken breasts

Salt and freshly ground black pepper, to taste

2 eggs, beaten

Combine sauce ingredients in a saucepan, and bring to a boil over high heat. Reduce to low. Simmer for 10 minutes until mixture is reduced by half. Remove, cool to room temperature, blend smooth, and reserve.

Preheat oven to 400°F.

Add pistachios, panko, paprika and salt in a food processor. Pulse until mixture resembles small breadcrumbs. Pour onto a plate, and reserve.

Season the chicken breasts with salt and pepper. Dip chicken breasts in beaten egg, coating it on all sides. Place in the pistachio breading and very firmly press the coating onto both sides.

Place the chicken breasts on a wire rack atop a baking sheet. Place in the oven, and bake for 20 minutes. Remove, and allow chicken to rest for 5 minutes before serving with the sauce.

This casserole is just crying out to be prepared in a slow cooker—fry the chicken, sauté the onions, then put all the ingredients into your crockpot. It'll cook to perfection throughout the day.

chicken, tomato and onion casserole

serves 4

1½ tablespoons unsalted butter

2 tablespoons olive oil

One chicken (4 pounds), skinned, bone in, and cut into 8 pieces

2 red onions, sliced

2 garlic cloves, finely chopped

One 14.5-ounce can tomatoes, chopped

2 tablespoons chopped fresh flat-leaf parsley

6 fresh basil leaves, torn

1 tablespoon sun-dried tomato paste

²/₃ cup red wine

Salt and freshly ground pepper, to taste

1 cup mushrooms, sliced

Preheat the oven to 325°F.

Melt the butter with the olive oil in a Dutch oven or flameproof casserole. Add the chicken pieces and fry, turning frequently for about 10 minutes, or until golden brown. Using a slotted spoon, transfer the chicken pieces to a platter.

Add the onions and garlic to the casserole, and cook over low heat, stirring occasionally, for 10 minutes, or until the onions become translucent. Add the tomatoes with their juice, parsley, basil leaves, tomato paste, and wine, and season to taste with salt and pepper. Bring to a boil, and then return the chicken pieces to the casserole, pushing them down into the sauce.

Cover and cook in the oven for 50 minutes. Add the mushrooms, and cook for an additional 10 minutes, until the mushrooms are warmed through. Serve immediately.

A great recipe for using up those winter squash. The chorizo adds an unexpected layer of flavor and texture.

chicken, pumpkin and chorizo casserole

serves 4

3 tablespoons olive oil

One chicken (5 pounds), cut into 8 pieces and dusted with flour

8 ounces (1 cup) fresh chorizo sausage, thickly sliced

3 tablespoons chopped fresh sage

1 onion, chopped

6 garlic cloves, peeled and sliced

2 celery stalks, sliced

1 small sugar pumpkin or butternut squash, peeled and coarsely chopped

1 cup dry sherry

2½ cups chicken broth

One 14.5-ounce can chopped tomatoes

2 bay leaves

Salt and freshly ground pepper, to taste

3-4 tablespoons chopped fresh flat-leaf parsley

Preheat the oven to 350°F.

Heat the oil in a Dutch oven or flameproof casserole, and fry the chicken with the chorizo and sage leaves until golden-brown. Remove the meat with a slotted spoon and reserve. (You may need to do this in batches.)

Add the onion, garlic, celery, and pumpkin or squash to the casserole, and cook until the vegetables begin to brown slightly. Add the sherry, chicken broth, tomatoes, and bay leaves, and season with salt and pepper, to taste.

Return the reserved chicken, chorizo, and sage to the casserole, cover, and cook in the oven for 1 hour. Remove the casserole from the oven, uncover, stir in the parsley, and serve.

chicken, tomato and onion casserole

page 244

chicken, pumpkin and
chorizo casserole
❖
page 245

The unusual crust, incorporating subtle herbs and tangy feta cheese, lifts this dish out of the mundane and into the realms of the sublime.

chicken casserole with herb crust

serves 4

1 tablespoon olive oil

1 tablespoon unsalted butter

4 whole (drumstick and thigh) chicken legs, dusted in flour

1 onion, chopped

3 garlic cloves, sliced

4 parsnips, peeled and cut into large chunks

1 cup dry white wine

3½ cups chicken broth

3 leeks, white parts only, trimmed, sliced, and thoroughly washed

3 ounces prunes, halved (optional)

1 tablespoon Dijon mustard

1 tablespoon mixed dried herbs

Salt and freshly ground pepper, to taste

½ cup fresh breadcrumbs

2 ounces (¼ cup) feta cheese, crumbled

2 tablespoons chopped fresh tarragon

2 tablespoons chopped fresh flat-leaf parsley

Preheat oven to 350°F.

In a Dutch oven or flameproof casserole, melt the olive oil and butter together, then fry the chicken until it is golden brown. Remove with a slotted spoon, and keep warm.

Add the onion, garlic, and parsnips to the casserole, and cook until the vegetables are slightly browned. Add the wine, chicken broth, leeks, prunes (if using), mustard, and mixed herbs. Season with salt and pepper, to taste. Return the chicken to the casserole, cover, and bake for 1 hour.

Mix the breadcrumbs, feta cheese, and herbs together in a bowl.

Remove the casserole from the oven and increase the oven temperature to 400°F. Sprinkle the breadcrumb mixture over the chicken, and return the casserole to the oven, uncovered, for 10 minutes or until the crust starts to brown slightly. Remove from the oven, and serve immediately.

Chicken with apples? Different, to say the least, even unexpected—and completely irresistible!

chicken and apple pot

serves 4

Four 6-ounce boneless, skinless chicken breasts

1 tablespoon olive oil

1 onion, chopped

2 celery stalks, coarsely chopped

1½ tablespoons all-purpose flour

1¼ cups apple juice

2/3 cup chicken stock

3 apples (Gala or Golden Delicious) peeled, cored, 1 quartered, and 2 sliced

2 bay leaves

1–2 teaspoons honey

Salt and freshly ground pepper, to taste

1 yellow bell pepper, seeded and cut into chunks

1 tablespoon unsalted butter

2 tablespoons firmly packed light brown sugar

1 tablespoon chopped fresh mint, to garnish

Preheat the oven to 375°F.

Lightly rinse the chicken, and pat dry with paper towels.

Heat the oil in a deep skillet, and cook the chicken over medium-high heat, turning frequently, for 10 minutes, or until golden and sealed. Using a slotted spoon, transfer the chicken to an ovenproof casserole.

Add the onion and celery to the skillet, and cook over medium heat, stirring frequently, for 5 minutes, or until softened. Sprinkle in the flour and cook, stirring constantly, for 2 minutes, then remove from the heat.

Gradually stir in the apple juice and stock, then return to the heat and bring to a boil, stirring constantly. Add the quartered apple, bay leaves, and honey, and season to taste with salt and pepper.

Pour the sauce over the chicken in the casserole, then cover and bake for for 25 minutes. Add the bell pepper, and cook for an additional 10–15 minutes, or until the chicken is tender and the juices run clear when a skewer is inserted into the thickest part of the meat.

To prepare the remaining apples, preheat the broiler to high. Melt the butter in a pan over low heat. Line the broiler pan with aluminum foil. Brush the apple slices with half the butter, then sprinkle with a little brown sugar and cook under the broiler for 2–3 minutes, or until the sugar has caramelized. Turn the slices over. Brush with the remaining butter, and sprinkle with the remaining sugar, and cook for an additional 2 minutes. Serve the stew garnished with the apple slices and mint.

The pastrami sandwich meets the buffalo chicken wing in this tasty party snack. No blue cheese dressing here — since these chicken wings are rubbed with pastrami spices, they're served with Russian or Thousand Island dressing.

pastrami spice-rubbed chicken wings

makes about 20 wings

¼ cup white vinegar

1 tablespoon granulated sugar

2 teaspoons kosher salt (or 1¼ teaspoon fine table salt), plus additional 1 teaspoon, or as needed

2½ pounds chicken-wing sections

2 tablespoons coarsely ground black pepper

2 teaspoons all-purpose flour

1½ tablespoons ground coriander

1 tablespoon smoked paprika

½ teaspoon dry mustard

Pinch of cayenne pepper

Combine vinegar, sugar, and 2 teapoons kosher salt in a bowl, and mix to dissolve. Add the chicken wings, and toss until evenly coated. Refrigerate for 2 hours, tossing occasionally. Drain the chicken wings well, and pat dry with paper towels.

Add wings to a large mixing bowl, and sprinkle over the black pepper, flour, coriander, paprika, mustard, and cayenne. Season with 1 teaspoon salt, and toss wings to completely and evenly coat with the spices.

Preheat oven to 425°F.

Transfer the wings to baking sheet that's been greased or lined with a silicon mat. Bake for 20 minutes, remove, and turn each wing over. Bake another 20 minutes, or until the chicken wings are browned and cooked all the way through. When done, the bones will easily pull out from the wings.

Serve hot with Russian or Thousand Island dressing.

Not exactly an authentic recipe, but amazingly delicious and perfect for large groups.

chicken enchiladas

makes 12 enchiladas

1 onion, chopped

2 tablespoons vegetable oil

One 7-ounce can chopped green chiles

½ teaspoon black pepper

1 tablespoon chile powder

2 teaspoon cumin

½ teaspoon dried oregano

4 cups shredded chicken (picked from a large cooked chicken)

1 teaspoon salt

½ cup water

1 cup sour cream

3 cups shredded Monterey Jack cheese, divided

2 cups ricotta cheese

One 28-ounce can red enchilada sauce

Twelve 9-inch flour tortillas

¼ cup chopped cilantro (optional), to garnish

Preheat oven to 350°F.

In a large skillet, on medium heat, sauté onion in the oil until translucent. Reduce heat to low. Add green chiles, pepper, chile powder, cumin, oregano, chicken, half the salt, and water to the skillet. Mix thoroughly, and remove from heat.

In a mixing bowl, combine sour cream, 2 cups of Monterey Jack cheese, ricotta cheese, and remaining salt. Mix until blended.

Pour ¼ cup of enchilada sauce in the bottom of 11x14 casserole dish. Distribute the chicken mixture and cheese mixture evenly in the center of each of the tortillas. Roll up and place filled tortillas in pan, seam side down. Pour over remaining sauce, and top with remaining Monterey Jack cheese.

Bake for 40–50 minutes, or until bubbly and browned. Allow to cool for 10 minutes. Garnish with cilantro, if using.

What's more fun to eat than a tasty chicken drumstick? How about eating a tasty chicken drumstick that's covered with a thick, glistening barbecue glaze?

memphis drumsticks

makes 12 drumsticks

12 chicken drumsticks, about 3½ pounds

1 cup barbecue sauce, divided

1 tablespoon brown sugar

1 tablespoon cider vinegar

1 teaspoon salt, plus more as needed

½ teaspoon freshly ground black pepper

½ teaspoon hot sauce

Vegetable oil, to grease pan

With a sharp knife, make 2 slashes, about 1-inch apart, into the thickest part of the drumstick, cutting to the bone. Transfer the chicken to a large sealable plastic freezer bag.

In a small bowl, mix together ¼ cup of the barbecue sauce with the rest of the ingredients. Pour into the bag of chicken, press out most of the air, and seal tightly. Shake the bag gently to distribute the sauce evenly. Refrigerate for at least 4 hours.

Preheat oven to 400°F.

Line a baking sheet with foil and grease lightly with vegetable oil. Remove the chicken from the bag with tongs, and space evenly on the pan. Discard the contents of the bag. Brush both sides of the drumsticks with barbecue sauce.

Bake for 15 minutes, remove, and brush generously with more barbecue sauce. Return chicken to the oven, and repeat this brushing process 3 more times, for a total cooking time of about 50–60 minutes. When done, the chicken will be fork-tender.

chicken enchiladas

❖

page 254

memphis drumsticks

page 255

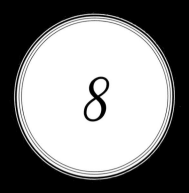

8

GRILLED CHICKEN

This satisfying recipe is full of flavor and very nutritious. The contrast between the hot chicken and the cool, savory salad makes for a great plate of food.

chicken breasts with lentils and arugula

serves 4

For the chicken breasts:

4 boneless, skinless chicken breasts

2 tablespoon olive oil

4 cloves garlic, roughly chopped

1 tablespoon dried Italian herb mix (usually rosemary, thyme, basil, oregano, marjoram)

1 teaspoon fresh ground black pepper

Salt, to taste

Juice from ½ lemon

For the salad:

2 cups cooked lentils, drained, cooled

2 tablespoon olive oil

¼ cup rice vinegar

1 tablespoon Dijon mustard

Juice from ½ lemon

Salt and freshly ground black pepper, to taste

4 cups arugula leaves, washed, dried, roughly chopped

Lemon wedges to garnish, optional

Combine all the chicken ingredients in a plastic bag, and shake to combine. Refrigerate for 2 to 8 hours to marinate.

Add the lentils, olive oil, vinegar, mustard, lemon, salt and pepper to a mixing bowl; mix well to combine. Just before serving, fold in the arugula, and divide salad on four plates.

Remove chicken from marinade and remove any pieces of garlic. Season the chicken with additional salt if desired. On a hot, preheated grill pan, cook for about 5 minutes per side, or until done. Top the lentils and arugula with the chicken breasts, and serve with lemon wedges.

This technique for barbecue chicken makes for a really juicy bird. As the chicken is cooked most of the way with the skin side up on the grill, the sauce can cook without being burned by the grill's flames.

backyard barbecue chicken

serves 4

1 whole chicken, split in half, wing tips removed

2 tablespoon rice vinegar

2 cloves garlic, mashed

¾ cup prepared barbecue sauce, divided

For the dry rub:

2 teaspoons kosher salt

1 teaspoon freshly ground black pepper

1 teaspoon paprika

1 teaspoon brown sugar

With a sharp knife, make several deep cuts through the skin and flesh of the chicken—two across the breast, two across the thigh, one across each leg. In a bowl, combine the vinegar, garlic, and ¼ cup of the barbecue sauce. Add the chicken halves and toss to coat in the marinade. Once coated, turn the chicken skin-side down in the bowl, cover, and refrigerate for 3 hours.

Remove the chicken from the marinade, and pat dry with paper towels. Mix together the dry-rub ingredients and sprinkle over both sides of the chicken.

Build a medium fire with your charcoal. Brush the grates lightly with oil, and place the chicken skin-side down on the grill. Cook for just 3–4 minutes to create some grill marks, then turn over so the skin side is up. Brush the top of the chicken generously with barbecue sauce. Cover the grill, and cook, without turning the chicken again, for 40 minutes, or until internal temperature is 165°F. While the chicken is grilling, brush more barbecue sauce on every 10 minutes.

This brightly flavored Southwestern-style recipe is the perfect antidote for the boring boneless, skinless chicken breast.

spicy lime-chipotle chicken breasts

serves 6

6 large boneless, skinless chicken breasts

¼ cup fresh lime juice

¼ cup orange juice

4 garlic cloves, crushed fine

1½ teaspoons chipotle chile powder

1 teaspoon smoked paprika

1 teaspoon cumin

2 tablespoons vegetable oil

Salt, to taste

Fresh lime wedges (optional), for serving

Use a sharp knife to score the top of the chicken breast in a crisscross pattern with ⅛-inch deep cuts, spaced about every half-inch.

Add all the ingredients except the chicken and salt into a mixing bowl. Whisk to combine thoroughly. Add the chicken, and toss to coat. Pour the contents into a large zip-top plastic freezer bag, seal, and marinate in the refrigerator for 3–6 hours.

Transfer the chicken breasts to a plate. Pat the chicken lightly with paper towels to remove excess liquid. Brush with a little vegetable oil, and season generously with salt. If so desired, more chipotle may be added at this point for a spicier version.

Cook the breasts on a preheated charcoal grill for 5–7 minutes per side, or until cooked through. These may also be done on a gas grill or a stovetop grill pan. Serve the chicken breasts topped with wedges of fresh lime, if desired.

How can such a simple marinade pack so much of a flavor punch? Who knows? You'll just be glad it does when you get all those rave reviews.

grilled miso-ginger chicken breasts

serves 4

¼ cup white miso paste

¹/₃ cup rice-wine vinegar

2 tablespoons honey

2 tablespoons lime juice

1 tablespoon soy sauce

1 tablespoon minced ginger

4 boneless, skinless chicken breasts

1 tablespoon vegetable oil

Combine all ingredients, except chicken and oil, in a plastic freezer bag. Add chicken, and shake to coat. Marinate in refrigerator for 2 hours.

Remove chicken from marinade, and place on a plate. Boil reserved marinade for 1 minute, and save for basting.

Preheat the grill over medium-high heat. Once preheated, brush grill with oil. Grill chicken for 6–8 minutes per side, or until cooked through. Toward the end of the cooking time, brush the breasts with remaining marinade to glaze. Remove the chicken from the grill, and let it rest for 5 minutes before serving.

This is not your parents' grilled chicken. The mint and apricot make for a great sweet and tangy glaze that can be used on any cut of chicken, if breasts aren't your thing.

grilled chicken breasts
with mint-apricot glaze

serves 4

4 pounds boneless, skinless chicken breasts

Salt and freshly ground black pepper, to taste

½ cup peach nectar

6 tablespoons apricot preserves

4 tablespoons chopped fresh mint

1 tablespoon olive oil

1 tablespoon sherry vinegar

½ teaspoon curry powder

2 clove garlic, minced

2 green onions, chopped

1 tablespoon Dijon mustard

½ teaspoon salt

Season chicken with salt and pepper.

In a bowl combine ¼ cup peach nectar, 2 tablespoons preserves, 2 tablespoons mint, olive oil, vinegar, curry, and garlic. Pour into a large plastic freezer bag and add the chicken. Seal bag, and shake to coat. Marinate in the refrigerator for 3 hours.

Remove chicken from marinade, and wipe off excess marinade. Season with salt and pepper to taste, and grill chicken directly over a medium charcoal fire until chicken cooked through, or reaches an internal temperature of 160°F.

In a mixing bowl, combine rest of nectar, preserves, mint, green onions, mustard, mustard, and salt to taste. Drizzle chicken with sauce, and serve immediately.

Using the flavors traditionally found in Italian sausage, this chicken will get rave reviews at your next backyard cookout.

garlic, fennel and orange grilled chicken

serves 6

12 boneless, skinless chicken thighs (may substitute halved chicken breasts)

4 cloves garlic, crushed

¼ cup orange juice

2 teaspoons orange zest

1½ tablespoons kosher salt

1 tablespoon dried Italian herb mix

1 tablespoon paprika

1 tablespoon freshly ground black pepper

2 tablespoons fennel seed, cracked and crushed slightly with flat of a knife

1 tablespoon olive oil

Combine ingredients in a mixing bowl, and toss to combine completely. (Massaging in with your hands is the best method.) Transfer to a large plastic freezer bag, and refrigerate at least 4 hours, or overnight.

Set up your grill for direct cooking over medium heat. Brush grates lightly with oil when ready to cook. Remove chicken from marinade, place on preheated grill, and cook for 7–8 minutes per side, or until cooked through.

grilled chicken breasts
with mint-apricot glaze
❧
page 268

garlic, fennel and orange
grilled chicken
❖
page 269

Yogurt has been used as a marinade for chicken for centuries. The tangy marinade keeps the chicken tender and moist.

yogurt-marinated chicken breasts

serves 4

½ cup plain Greek yogurt, or any plain yogurt

Juice of 1 lemon

2 teaspoons lemon zest

1 tablespoon paprika

1 teaspoon dried thyme

½ teaspoon dried rosemary

1 teaspoon salt

1 teaspoon freshly ground black pepper

4 cloves garlic, crushed

1 tablespoon olive oil

4 boneless, skinless chicken breasts

Whisk together all the marinade ingredients in a large bowl, and add in the chicken breasts. Toss to completely coat the chicken with the marinade. Cover and refrigerate for at least 4 hours, up to overnight.

Remove chicken from marinade, wiping off any excess. Season with additional salt and pepper, to taste, if desired. Grill or broil chicken for about 5–6 minutes per side, depending on size, or until an internal temperature of 165°F is reached.

The fruity sweetness of the raspberry jam and tangy balsamic vinegar works so well with these smoky, grilled chicken breasts.

grilled chicken breasts
with raspberry-balsamic sauce

serves 4

¼ cup raspberry jam

1 tablespoon balsamic vinegar

1 teaspoon chopped fresh thyme leaves

¼ cup chicken broth

4 boneless, skinless chicken breasts

1 teaspoon vegetable oil

Salt and freshly ground black pepper

Combine jam, balsamic vinegar, fresh thyme, and broth in small saucepan, and stir to combine. Place over medium heat. Cook, stirring, until the mixture begins to simmer. Remove from heat and reserve.

Pat chicken breasts dry with paper towels, and brush with oil. Season with salt and pepper on both sides. Preheat grill on medium-high. Lightly oil grates, and cook the chicken for about 5–7 minutes per side, until cooked through, or until a thermometer reads 165°F internal temperature.

Transfer chicken to a plate, cover loosely with foil, and let it rest about 5 minutes before serving with the raspberry-balsamic sauce spooned over.

This backyard favorite is especially good served over a tossed green salad. The flavorful juices from the chicken and marinade combine to make its own kind of warm dressing.

grilled balsamic-rosemary-lemon chicken

serves 4

½ cup balsamic vinegar

¼ cup olive oil

2 tablespoons freshly minced rosemary leaves

4 cloves minced garlic

2 tablespoons freshly grated lemon zest

2 teaspoons red chile flakes

8 boneless, skinless chicken thighs or 4 chicken breasts

Salt and freshly ground pepper, to taste

Combine the balsamic vinegar, olive oil, rosemary, garlic, lemon zest and red chile flakes in a plastic freezer bag. Place the chicken in bag and tightly seal. Shake to ensure chicken is evenly coated. Refrigerate, turning occasionally, for 4–6 hours.

Remove chicken from the marinade and pat dry. Season the chicken generously with salt and pepper. Preheat a grill over medium, and then brush grates lightly with oil. Place chicken on the grill and cook for about 7 minutes per side, or until the chicken is cooked through. Serve immediately.

Perfect for a summer barbecue or for under the broiler, these kebobs have a marinade sauce that is packed with flavor.

spicy chicken and tomato kebobs

1 pound boneless, skinless chicken breasts

3 tablespoons tomato paste

2 tablespoons honey

2 tablespoons Worcestershire or steak sauce

1 tablespoon chopped fresh rosemary

16 cherry tomatoes

Using a sharp knife, cut the chicken into 1-inch chunks and place in a bowl. Mix the tomato paste, honey, Worcestershire sauce, and rosemary together in a separate bowl. Add sauce to the chicken, stirring to coat evenly.

Preheat the barbecue or broiler.

Thread the chicken pieces and cherry tomatoes alternately onto 8 metal or presoaked wooden skewers.

Cook the kebobs over medium-hot coals or under the preheated broiler, turning occasionally, for 8–10 minutes, until the chicken is cooked through.

Transfer to a large serving plate, and serve immediately.

Chicken breast meat can sometimes dry out on the barbecue or under the broiler—the rich marinade, combined with the long marinating time, ensures that these kebobs are moist and full of flavor.

zesty chicken kebobs

serves 6–8

4 boneless, skinless chicken breasts (about 6 ounces each)

Juice and zest of ½ lemon

Juice and zest of ½ orange

2 tablespoons honey

2 tablespoons olive oil

2 tablespoons chopped fresh mint

¼ teaspoon ground coriander

Salt and freshly ground black pepper, to taste

Using a sharp knife, cut the chicken into 1-inch cubes, and then place in a large glass bowl.

Place the lemon and orange juices, zest, honey, oil, mint, and coriander in a measuring cup and mix together. Season to taste with salt and pepper.

Pour the marinade over the chicken, and toss until thoroughly coated. Cover with plastic wrap, and let marinate in the refrigerator for up to 8 hours.

Preheat the barbecue or broiler. Drain the chicken, reserving the marinade. Thread the chicken onto 8 metal or presoaked wooden skewers.

Cook the skewers over medium-hot coals or under the preheated broiler, turning and basting frequently with the reserved marinade, for 6–10 minutes, or until cooked through. Transfer to a large serving plate, and serve immediately.

spicy chicken and tomato kebobs

❧

page 278

zesty chicken kebobs

page 279

It's a proven fact: People love grilled meat on a stick, or, in this case, a skewer. Here we are using an easy-to-make ranch-dressing marinade to create some very juicy results.

rosemary-ranch chicken kebobs

serves 4

¼ cup ranch dressing

¼ cup olive oil

2 tablespoons rice vinegar

½ teaspoon hot sauce

1 tablespoon Worcestershire sauce

2 tablespoons minced fresh rosemary leaves

1 teaspoon salt

½ teaspoon black pepper

4 boneless, skinless chicken breasts, cut into 2-inch pieces

Whisk together all the marinade ingredients in a mixing bowl. Add chicken, and mix until pieces are well coated. Cover and refrigerate for at least 2 hours.

Preheat grill to medium-high heat. Remove chicken from marinade, and thread chicken onto 4 long metal skewers. Lightly oil grates. Grill kebobs for 10–2 minutes, or until cooked through.

Serve up a meal with an authentic Caribbean flavor with this delicious jerk-seasoned chicken dish.

jerk chicken

serves 4

2 red chiles

2 tablespoons corn oil, plus extra for brushing

2 garlic cloves, finely chopped

1 tablespoon finely chopped onion

1 tablespoon finely chopped green onion

1 tablespoon white-wine vinegar

1 tablespoon lime juice

2 teaspoon raw brown sugar

1 teaspoon dried thyme

1 teaspoon ground cinnamon

1 teaspoon ground allspice

¼ teaspoon freshly grated nutmeg

4 chicken quarters

Salt and pepper

Sprigs of fresh cilantro and lime wedges, to garnish

Seed and finely chop the chiles, then place them in a small nonmetallic bowl with the oil, garlic, onion, green onion, vinegar, lime juice, raw brown sugar, thyme, cinnamon, allspice, and nutmeg. Season to taste with salt and pepper and mash thoroughly with a fork.

Using a sharp knife, make a series of diagonal slashes in the chicken quarters and place them in a large nonmetallic dish. Spoon the jerk seasoning over the chicken, rubbing it well into the slashes. Cover and let marinate in the refrigerator for up to 8 hours.

Preheat the broiler or grill. Remove the meat from the marinade, discarding the marinade. Brush with oil and cook under the preheated broiler, or over a medium hot grill turning frequently, for 30–35 minutes, until the juices run clear when a sharp knife is inserted into the thickest part of the meat. Transfer to plates and serve immediately, garnished with sprigs of cilantro and lime wedges.

9

THE PERFECT SIDE DISHES

The secret of perfect roast potatoes is simple: hot, hot, hot fat and a quick shake of a saucepan. Perfect roast potatoes guaranteed!

roasted potatoes

serves 6

3 pounds large potatoes, peeled and cut into even chunks

3 tablespoons pan drippings, goose fat, duck fat, or olive oil

Salt, to taste

Preheat the oven to 425°F.

Bring a large saucepan of lightly salted water to the boil, add the potatoes, and cook over medium heat, covered, for 5–7 minutes. They will still be firm. Remove from the heat.

Meanwhile, add the drippings, fat, or oil to a roasting pan and place in the preheated oven.

Drain the potatoes well and return them to the pan. Cover with the lid and firmly shake the pan so that the surface of the potatoes is roughened to help give a much crisper texture.

Remove the roasting pan from the oven and carefully put the potatoes into the hot fat. Baste them to ensure they are all coated with the fat.

Roast at the top of the oven for 45–50 minutes, until they are browned all over and thoroughly crisp. Turn and baste again only once during the cooking process or the crunchy edges will be destroyed.

Carefully transfer the potatoes from the roasting pan into a warmed serving dish. Sprinkle with a little salt, and serve immediately.

A simple lemon-and-brown-sugar glaze is all that's needed to bring out the yam's natural earthy sweetness.

glazed yams

serves 6

Juice of 1 lemon

2½ pounds garnet or other orange-fleshed yams

2 tablespoons unsalted butter

¼ cup packed brown sugar

½ teaspoon salt, or to taste

⅛ teaspoon cayenne pepper

Preheat oven to 350°F.

Add the lemon juice to a large mixing bowl. Peel yams, cut into 1-inch cubes, and toss with the lemon juice.

Melt the butter in a large skillet over medium-high heat. Add the yams and lemon juice, brown sugar, salt, and cayenne. Cook, stirring, for about 5–7 minutes, until a sticky syrup is formed and the edges of the yams begin to caramelize.

Remove from heat, and transfer into a lightly buttered, ovenproof baking dish. Bake for 20–25 minutes, or until tender. Serve hot.

It's not really Spring until you see bright green plates of asparagus on the table.

asparagus with lemon butter sauce

serves 4

2 pounds asparagus spears, trimmed

1 tablespoon olive oil

Salt and pepper

For the sauce:

Juice of 1 lemon

2 tablespoons water

8 tablespoons unsalted butter, cut into cubes

Preheat oven to 400°F.

Lay the asparagus spears out in a single layer on a large baking sheet. Drizzle over the oil, season to taste with salt and pepper and roast in the pre-heated oven for 10 minutes, or until just tender.

Meanwhile, make the sauce. Pour the lemon juice into a saucepan and add the water. Heat for a minute or so, then slowly add the butter, cube by cube, stirring constantly until it has all been incorporated.

Season to taste with pepper and serve immediately, drizzled over the asparagus.

This rich, decadent green-bean casserole is strictly for those special-occasion meals where counting calories is not even a remote consideration.

green-bean casserole

serves 6–8

1½ pounds green beans, trimmed and cut into thirds

1½ cups heavy cream

½ cup chicken broth

1 garlic clove, minced fine

½ teaspoon salt

¼ teaspoon freshly ground black pepper

Pinch of nutmeg

One 6-ounce can french-fried onions, divided

Preheat oven to 375°F.

Bring a pot of well-salted water to boil. Blanch the beans in the boiling water for 5 minutes. Drain very well, and reserve.

Add the cream, broth, garlic, salt, pepper and nutmeg to a small saucepan. Place over medium heat and cook, stirring occasionally, until the mixture comes to a simmer. Remove from heat, and reserve.

Spread half the french-fried onions in the bottom of a 2-quart casserole dish. Spread the beans evenly over the onions. Pour over the cream mixture. Use a fork to press the beans down into the cream. Top with the other half of the fried onions. Use a fork to flatten the top, pressing down firmly.

Bake for 25–30 minutes, or until the beans are very tender, and the casserole is browned and bubbling. Remove, and let rest for 15 minutes before serving.

Artichokes are so naturally delicious, and this simple roasting technique concentrates the flavors even more.

roasted artichokes

serves 6

6 whole large artichokes

3 lemons, halved

6 cloves garlic, peeled and left whole

6 tablespoons olive oil

Salt, to taste

Using a serrated knife, cut off the stem of the artichoke where it meets the base. Turn the artichoke around and cut off 1 inch of the top. Quickly rub each artichoke with a cut lemon so it doesn't discolor.

Tear off 4 square pieces of foil. Rub a few drops of olive oil on the foil and place an artichoke stem-side down. Use your fingers to loosen the leaves in the center. Stick a clove of garlic into the center and push down an inch or so. Sprinkle over a large pinch of salt. Drizzle 1 tablespoon of olive oil over the top. Finish by squeezing the half lemon over the top. The lemon juice will "wash" the salt and olive down in between the leaves.

Gather up the corners of the foil, and press together on top to tightly seal the artichoke (like a chocolate kiss). Wrap in a second piece of foil to form a tight seal.

Repeat with the other artichokes. Place in a roasting pan and bake at 425°F for 1 hour and 15 minutes. Let rest for 15 minutes before unwrapping and serving.

Can be eaten hot, warm, or chilled.

THE PERFECT SIDE DISHES

Almost everyone loves smooth, creamy mashed potatoes, but they can't be lumpy. A potato masher is invaluable, but I prefer a potato ricer, which presses the potato through tiny holes and makes fine "worms," which means you never get lumps.

perfect mashed potatoes

serves 4

2 pounds potatoes, such as russet

4 tablespoons unsalted butter

3 tablespoons whole milk

Salt and pepper, to taste

Peel the potatoes, placing them in cold water as you prepare the others to prevent them from turning brown.

Cut the potatoes into even-sized chunks, and cook in a large saucepan of boiling salted water over a medium heat, covered, for 20–25 minutes until they are tender. Test with the point of a knife right to the middle, in order to avoid lumps.

Remove the pan from the heat, and drain the potatoes. Return the potatoes to the hot pan, and mash with a potato masher until smooth.

Add the butter, and continue to mash until it is all mixed in. Add the milk.

Taste the mash, and season with salt and pepper, to taste. Serve immediately.

Variations: For herb mash, mix in 3 tablespoons chopped fresh parsley, thyme or mint. For mustard or horseradish mash, mix in 2 tablespoons whole-grain mustard or horseradish sauce. For pesto mash, stir in ¼ cup fresh pesto. For nutmeg mash, grate ½ a nutmeg into the mash and add ½ cup plain natural yogurt. To make creamed potato, add ½ cup sour cream and 2 tablespoons snipped fresh chives.

Roasting in a very hot oven really brings out the natural sweetness in vegetables and intensifies their flavor.

roasted root vegetables

serves 4–6

3 parsnips, cut into 2-inch chunks

4 baby turnips, quartered

3 carrots, cut into 2-inch chunks

1 pound butternut squash, peeled and cut into 2-inch chunks

1 pound sweet potatoes, peeled and cut into 2-inch chunks

2 garlic cloves, finely chopped

2 tablespoons chopped fresh rosemary

2 tablespoons chopped fresh thyme

2 teaspoons chopped fresh sage

3 tablespoons olive oil

Salt and reshly ground pepper, to taste

2 tablespoons chopped fresh mixed herbs, such as flat-leaf parsley, thyme, and mint, to garnish

Preheat the oven to 425°F.

Arrange all the vegetables in a single layer in a large roasting pan. Sprinkle over the garlic and the herbs. Pour the oil over the vegetables, and season well with salt and pepper.

Toss all the ingredients together until they are well mixed and coated with the oil (you can let them marinate at this stage so that the flavors can be absorbed).

Roast the vegetables at the top of the preheated oven for 50–60 minutes, until they are cooked and nicely browned. Turn the vegetables over halfway through the cooking time.

Serve with a good handful of fresh herbs sprinkled on top and a final seasoning of salt and pepper, to taste.

perfect mashed potatoes

❖

page 296

roasted root vegetables

page 297

Red cabbage absorbs new flavors extremely well, and the addition of the vinegar makes this a delicious side dish.

braised red cabbage and apples

serves 6

1 teaspoon whole caraway seeds

1 tablespoon vegetable oil

1 red onion, halved and thinly sliced

2 tablespoons brown sugar

1 small red cabbage, shredded

2 apples, peeled and thinly sliced

2 tablespoons red wine

1/2 cup apple juice

2 tablespoons cider vinegar

Salt and freshly ground black pepper, to taste

1 teaspoon lemon juice

In a saucepan over medium heat, dry roast the caraway seeds for about 1 minute, until they start to give off an aroma.

Heat the oil in a large pot over medium heat, add the onion, and sauté for 5 minutes until it becomes translucent. Add the brown sugar, stir, and add the cabbage and apples. Stir for a few minutes until the cabbage wilts. Add in the red wine, apple juice, and vinegar. Add the toasted caraway seeds and salt and pepper, to taste. Bring the mixture to a boil, lower to a simmer, add the lemon juice, cover, and cook for 30 minutes.

Note: Braised cabbage is wonderful served with chicken, meat, or pork dishes.

You'll forget all about how nutritious fresh broccoli is when you see this crispy, bubbling, golden-brown beauty coming to the table.

cheesy broccoli gratin

serves 6

4 tablespoons unsalted butter

¼ cup all-purpose flour

2 cups cold whole milk

Pinch of nutmeg

Pinch of cayenne pepper

1 teaspoon fresh thyme leaves, chopped (optional)

8 ounces extra-sharp Cheddar cheese, shredded

½ teaspoon salt, or to taste

2 pounds fresh broccoli crowns, cut into 2-inch pieces

½ cup plain breadcrumbs

2 tablespoons melted unsalted butter

2 tablespoons grated Parmesan cheese

Preheat oven to 375°F.

Melt the butter in a saucepan over medium heat, and add the flour. Cook, stirring, for about 3 minutes (the mixture should begin to smell like cooked pie crust). Slowly whisk in the cold milk. Continue whisking until there are no visible lumps. Add the nutmeg, cayenne, and thyme. The sauce will thicken as it comes back to a simmer. Reduce the heat to low, and simmer, stirring occasionally, for 10 minutes.

Turn off the heat, and stir in the cheese. When all the cheese has melted into the sauce, season with salt, and reserve until needed.

Note: Sauce may be strained if you are concerned about lumps.

Bring a pot of salted water to a rapid boil. Add the broccoli and cook for about 5 minutes, or just until the stem ends begin to get tender. Do not overcook, as the broccoli will cook further in the oven. Drain very well (otherwise the gratin will be watery). Transfer to a large mixing bowl.

Pour over the cheese sauce, and fold with a spatula until the broccoli is completely coated with the sauce. Transfer into a lightly buttered 2-quart casserole dish, using the spatula to distribute evenly. In a small bowl, combine breadcrumbs, butter, and Parmesan. Sprinkle evenly over the top, and bake for 25 minutes, or until the top is browned and bubbly.

For those times when regular potatoes just won't do. This creamy, cheesy scoop of side-dish heaven looks great next to any meaty main course.

scalloped potatoes

serves 8

2 tablespoons unsalted butter, divided

1 tablesoon all-purpose flour

1 cup heavy cream

2 cups whole milk

1 teaspoon salt

Pinch of nutmeg

Pinch of white pepper

4 sprigs fresh thyme

2 garlic cloves, minced

4½ pounds russet potatoes, sliced thin

Salt and freshly ground black pepper, to taste

4 ounces grated Swiss gruyere or white Cheddar

Preheat oven to 375°F.

Use half the butter to grease a 15x10–inch baking dish.

Melt the rest of the butter in a saucepan over medium heat. Whisk in the flour, and cook, stirring constantly, for 2 minutes. Whisk in the cream and milk, and bring to a simmer. Add the salt, nutmeg, white pepper, thyme, and garlic. Reduce heat to low, and simmer for 5 minutes. Remove the thyme sprigs, and reserve.

Layer half the potatoes in the baking dish. Season generously with salt and pepper. Top with half of the milk mixture. Top with half the cheese. Repeat with the remaining potatoes, sauce, and cheese.

Bake for about 1 hour, or until the top is browned and the potatoes are tender. Let rest for 15 minutes before serving.

A recipe from medieval Britain, this classic recipe is perfect served hot or cold with poultry dishes.

bread sauce

serves 6–9

1 onion

12 cloves

1 bay leaf

6 black peppercorns

2½ cups whole milk

2 cups fresh white breadcrumbs

2 tablespoons unsalted butter

Salt and pepper, to taste

Whole nutmeg, for grating

2 tablespoons heavy cream (optional)

Make small holes in the onion using the point of a sharp knife or a skewer, and stick the cloves in them.

Put the onion, bay leaf, and peppercorns in a saucepan, and pour in the milk. Bring to a boil, then remove from the heat, cover, and set aside to infuse for 1 hour.

Discard the onion and bay leaf, and strain the milk to remove the peppercorns. Return the milk to the cleaned pan, and add the breadcrumbs.

Cook the sauce over very low heat for 4–5 minutes, until the breadcrumbs have swollen, and the sauce is thick.

Beat in the butter, and season well with salt and pepper and a good grating of nutmeg. Stir in the cream just before serving, if using.

This salad will look so tasty, you'll want to dive right in, but be sure to wait at least two hours to give the flavors a chance to develop fully.

roasted red potato salad

serves 6

2½ pounds small red potatoes, washed

For the dressing:
2 garlic cloves, finely minced
1 teaspoon Dijon mustard
Pinch of cayenne pepper
¼ cup white wine vinegar
⅔ cup olive oil

Salt and freshly ground black pepper, to taste
1 tablespoon chopped flat-leaf parsley
1 tablespoon chopped tarragon
1 tablespoon chopped chives
1 teaspoon minced thyme leaves
⅔ cup olive oil

Preheat oven to 400°F.

Place the potatoes in a roasting pan. Roast for 25–30 minutes, or until tender (time will vary depending on size).

While the potatoes are in the oven, make the dressing. Add the garlic, Dijon, cayenne, and vinegar to a large mixing bowl. Whisk in the oil, very slowly at first, pouring in a steady stream, until incorporated.

When the cooked potatoes are just cool enough to handle, cut in halves or quarters. Add and toss the warm potatoes in the dressing, along with salt and pepper, to taste. Let sit for 15 minutes. Add the herbs, and toss again.

Cover and refrigerate for at least 2 hours, or overnight. Toss well before serving, and taste for salt and pepper. Additional fresh herbs can be sprinkled over the top, if desired.

Unless you have a commercial deep-fryer in your kitchen, regular French fries are probably best left to the neighborhood burger joint. On the contrary, these crusty and delicious oven-roasted steak fries are easily made at home.

garlic-and-herb steak fries

makes 8 portions

4 medium russet potatoes, scrubbed and rinsed

3 tablespoons olive oil

4 cloves garlic, minced and mashed against the cutting board with the flat of a knife

½ teaspoon dried rosemary, crushed fine

½ teaspoon dried oregano

½ teaspoon dried thyme

½ teaspoon paprika

½ teaspoon freshly ground black pepper

1 teaspoon salt

Preheat oven to 425°F.

Cut each potato in half lengthwise. Cut each half, lengthwise, into 4 equally sized wedges. Add the potato wedges to a large mixing bowl with the rest of the ingredients. Toss to coat the potatoes evenly.

Line a sheet pan with foil. Place the potato wedges skin-side down on the foil. Be sure to space evenly so potatoes cook uniformly.

Bake for 35–40 minutes, or until well browned, crusty-edged, and tender. Serve immediately, sprinkled with more salt, if desired.

This is the traditional accompaniment for any roast poultry, but is particularly good with chicken and turkey. Take care not to overcook the sprouts!

brussels sprouts with chestnuts

serves 4

12 ounces Brussels sprouts, trimmed

3 tablespoons unsalted butter

3½ ounces canned whole chestnuts

Pinch of grated nutmeg

Salt and pepper, to taste

½ cup sliced almonds, to garnish

Bring a large saucepan of lightly salted water to a boil. Add the Brussels sprouts, and cook for 5 minutes. Drain thoroughly.

Melt the butter in a large saucepan over medium heat. Add the Brussels sprouts, and cook, stirring, for 3 minutes, then add the chestnuts and nutmeg.

Season with salt and pepper, to taste, and stir well. Cook for an additional 2 minutes, stirring, then remove from the heat.

Transfer to a warmed serving dish, scatter over the almonds, and serve.

Tip: If you can buy Brussels sprouts still attached to their long central stalk, so much the better. They'll keep fresh for longer that way.

This moist, crumbly version of America's oldest bread has a slight sweetness that makes it a perfect match for spicy foods. A warm, freshly cut wedge next to a steaming bowl of chili is a truly beautiful thing.

cornbread

serves 6

8 tablespoons unsalted butter, melted

²/₃ cup white granulated sugar

2 large eggs

1 cup buttermilk

½ teaspoon baking soda

1 cup all-purpose flour

1 cup yellow cornmeal

½ teaspoon salt

Extra butter, to grease the pan

Preheat oven to 375°F.

In a large mixing bowl, whisk together the melted butter and sugar. Add the eggs, and whisk until combined. Add the buttermilk and baking soda, and whisk to combine. Add the flour, cornmeal, and salt. Using a spatula, stir until just blended. Do not mix any longer than necessary.

Lightly grease a 10-inch cast-iron skillet with butter. Pour in the batter, and bake for about 35 minutes, or until a toothpick inserted in the center comes out clean. Let cool for at least 15 minutes before trying to cut.

This dish is the perfect way to use up any leftover zucchini you may have in the refrigerator.

zucchini fritters

makes 20–30 fritters

¾ cup self-rising flour

2 large eggs, beaten

¼ cup whole milk

1 large zucchini

2 tablespoons fresh thyme, plus extra to garnish

Salt and freshly ground black pepper, to taste

1 tablespoon oil

Sift the flour into a large bowl, and make a well in the center. Add the eggs to the well, and, using a wooden spoon, gradually draw in the flour. Slowly add the milk to the mixture, stirring continuously to form a thick batter.

Grate the zucchini over a few paper towels placed in a bowl to absorb some of the juices.

Add the zucchini, thyme, and salt and pepper, to taste, to the batter, and mix thoroughly, for about 1 minute.

Heat the oil in a large, heavy-bottom skillet. Taking 1 tablespoon of the batter for a medium fritter or ½ tablespoon of batter for a smaller fritter, spoon the mixture into the hot oil and cook, in batches, for 3–4 minutes on each side.

Remove the fritters with a slotted spoon, and drain thoroughly on paper towels. Keep each batch of fritters warm in the oven while making the rest.

Transfer to serving plates, and serve hot, garnished with thyme.

THE PERFECT SIDE DISHES

This is a modern take on a very old Native-American staple, and makes a great, colorful side dish for almost any meal.

succulent succotash

serves 8

1 tablespoon olive oil

½ tablespoon unsalted butter

½ yellow onion, diced

3 garlic cloves, minced

1 jalapeño or other small hot chile pepper, sliced

½ red bell pepper, diced

½ cup diced tomatoes (fresh, if available)

4 ounces green beans, cut in ½-inch pieces

1½ cups fresh or frozen corn

1 cup frozen baby lima beans, thawed

1 cup cubed green zucchini

½ teaspoon ground cumin

Pinch of cayenne pepper

¼ cup water

Salt and freshly ground black pepper, to taste

Place a large skillet over medium heat, and add the olive oil and butter. When the butter foams up, add the onions and a big pinch of salt. Sauté for about 5 minutes, or until the onions begin to soften and turn golden.

Add the garlic, jalapeño, and bell pepper; sauté for 3 minutes. Add the rest of the ingredients, and cook, stirring occasionally until the vegetables are tender. More liquid may be added if the mixture gets too dry. When done, taste for salt, and adjust the seasoning, if needed. Serve immediately.

This corn-custard recipe is light, but still rich and satisfying. Since it's so soft and creamy, texturally, it makes a great match for things like barbecue pork ribs, grilled steaks, and fried fish.

creamy corn custard

serves 8

3 cups corn kernels, fresh, or thawed frozen

1½ cups heavy cream

½ cup whole milk

1¼ teaspoons salt

Pinch of cayenne pepper

4 eggs

3 egg yolks

Eight 6-ounce ovenproof ramekins, buttered

Preheat oven to 325°F.

Add the corn, cream, milk, salt, and cayenne to a saucepan. Bring to a simmer over medium heat. Turn off heat and remove to cool slightly. Carefully pour into a blender, and puree until very smooth. Reserve.

Add the eggs and egg yolks to a mixing bowl, and whisk for 30 seconds. Slowly, a cup at a time, stir in the warm corn-custard mixture. When everything is combined, ladle the mixture into 8 well-buttered ramekins.

Fill a roasting pan or casserole dish with 1 inch of hot water, and place in the filled ramekins. Bake for 35 minutes, or until the corn custard is just set. Remove from the baking dish, and let cool for 15 minutes before serving.

The custard may be eaten out of the ramekins, or run a paring knife around the inside and turn over on to a plate for a fancier presentation.

INDEX